LEARNING STRATEGIES FOR POST-LITERACY AND CONTINUING EDUCATION IN ALGERIA, EGYPT AND KUWAIT

Outcomes of an International Research Project of the Unesco Institute for Education organized in co-operation with the German Commission for Unesco, Bonn

D1721926

© Unesco Institute for Education 1987

Feldbrunnenstrasse 58
D-2000 Hamburg 13
Federal Republic of Germany

ISBN 92 820 1045 7

Printed by
Niko Jessen, Lübecker Str. 124
D-2000 Hamburg 76, Tel. 25 43 97

uie studies on post-literacy and
continuing education **6**

LEARNING STRATEGIES FOR POST-LITERACY AND CONTINUING EDUCATION IN ALGERIA, EGYPT AND KUWAIT

Outcomes of an international
Research Project of the Unesco
Institute for Education organized
in co-operation with the German
Commission for Unesco, Bonn

R. H. DAVE, A. OUANE, A. M. RANAWEERA (editors)

With contributions from
A. FETNI; A. F. GALAL AND S. NASSAR;
Y. A. AL-SHARAH AND D. KHABBAS

**unesco institute for education
hamburg**

uie studies on post-literacy and continuing education

titles published in this series:

1. **Learning Strategies for Post-literacy and Continuing Education: A Cross-National Perspective.**
   by R. H. Dave, D. A. Perera and A. Ouane.
   With contributions from H. S. Bhola and Anil Bordia.
   ISBN 92 820 1038 4

2. **Learning Strategies for Post-literacy and Continuing Education in Mali, Niger, Senegal and Upper Volta.**
   With contributions from A. Ouane, O. Kané, F. Badiane and P. T. Ilboudo.
   ISBN 92 820 1039 2

3. **Learning Strategies for Post-literacy and Continuing Education in Kenya, Nigeria, Tanzania and United Kingdom.**
   With contributions from D. Macharia, C. O. Akinde, Z. J. Mpogolo and A. Stock.
   ISBN 92 820 1040 6

4. **Learning Strategies for Post-literacy and Continuing Education in China, India, Indonesia, Nepal, Thailand and Vietnam.**
   With contributions from Li Jiyuan; D. V. Sharma; A Iskandar, U. Sihombing et al.; L. N. Belbase; N. Suntornpithug and Le Son.
   ISBN 92 820 1041 4

5. **Learning Strategies for Post-literacy and Continuing Education in Brazil, Colombia, Jamaica and Venezuela.**
   With contributions from A. M. Coutinho, L. M. Carmo Chaves and V. Galvão; L. Hurtado; M. Moulton-Campbell and A. Valbuena Paz.
   ISBN 92 820 1042 2

6. **Learning Strategies for Post-literacy and Continuing Education in Algeria, Egypt and Kuwait.**
   With contributions from A. Fetni; A. F. Galal; Y. Al-Sharah and D. Khabbas.
   ISBN 92 820 1045 7

All edited by R. H. Dave, A. Ouane and D. A. Perera

CONTENTS

CHAPTER 2   LEARNING STRATEGIES FOR POST-LITERACY AND
             BASIC LEVEL EDUCATION IN EGYPT IN THE
             PERSPECTIVE OF LIFELONG EDUCATION

Abdel Fattah Galal and Sami Nassar

CHAPTER 3 DEVELOPMENT OF LEARNING STRATEGIES FOR
           LITERACY, POST-LITERACY AND CONTINUING
           EDUCATION IN KUWAIT

Yacoub A. Al-Sharah and Deeb Khabbas

FOREWORD

Since 1972, the Unesco Institute for Education (UIE) has been conducting basic as well as developmental research on the concept of lifelong education and its implications for educational reforms and development. The activities of the Institute have been specifically focused on practical implications of this concept for the goals and content of education, learning strategies, evaluation and teacher education, covering the broad spectrum of formal, nonformal and informal systems of learning. The needs of both developed and developing countries have been kept in view throughout the planning and conduct of these activities.

One of the important areas of application of the principles of lifelong education in developing countries is related to the programmes of post-literacy and continuing education. This book is an outcome of some of the Institute's work in this particular field.

It is important to note in this connection that a large number of developing countries have recently launched massive programmes of adult literacy on a national scale, complementary to efforts towards implementing the universalization of primary education for children of school-going age. These are indeed recommendable efforts towards the democratization of education despite the problems of financial and other resources.

It has, however, been observed that those neo-literate adults who acquire literacy through such programmes have great difficulty in retaining it, and some of them lapse back into illiteracy if timely follow-up measures are not taken. The same phenomenon of reversal has also been observed in the case of children who drop out of the formal school system prematurely. On the other hand, literacy is considered as an important step towards the process of lifelong education and the achievement of a better quality of life, not only for every individual but also for the family and the community. Hence, one important question that needs to be tackled is: *How does one enable neo-literate adults and out-of-school children to retain their literacy skills?* It is essential that those who once acquire basic skills of reading, writing and computation make them permanent by re-inforcement through post-literacy programmes.

The post-literacy programmes, however, are not just remedial measures to ensure the retention and stabilization of literacy skills. Especially when they are developed in the context of lifelong education and with the purpose of improving the quality of life of the individuals and their collectives, they call for the continuation of learning in a flexible manner, utilizing the recently acquired literacy skills, and for the application of this learning to the larger processes of development. Thus, what is required is to develop programmes of post-literacy and continuing education to fulfil three major goals, namely, (i) *retention* and *stabilization* of literacy skills, (ii) *continuation* of learning beyond initial literacy skills, and (iii) *application* of this learning for improving various aspects of personal, social and vocational life. Again, one of the most critical questions is: *How can this be done?*

In the light of these and other similar factors, the need to develop suitable programmes of post-literacy and continuing education has been keenly felt in all the countries engaged in literacy and mass education programmes. Responding to this situation, in 1980 the UIE initiated a major project of research and research-based training on the Development of Learning Strategies for Post-literacy and Continuing Education of Neo-literates in the Perspective of Lifelong Education.

In this respect, the broad framework of lifelong education proved very valuable, for example,

(1) in enabling programmes of literacy and post-literacy to be viewed as a *continuum* within *total* education aimed at reducing inequality and at increasing the degree of *democratization* in education;

(2) in advocating the acquisition of post-literacy
     and continuing education through not only the
     formal system but also the *nonformal* system
     and *informal* learning opportunities created by
     print as well as non-print media of both modern
     and traditional types;

(3) in emphasizing that learning strategies should
     be *flexible* and provide *alternative approaches*
     to suit individuals and their groups in their
     local conditions;

(4) in ensuring that learning strategies pay due
     attention to certain *groups with special needs*
     such as women, youth, etc.;

(5) in encouraging an increasing degree of *indepen-
     dent* and *self-directed* learning;

(6) in insisting that learning should be *inte-
     grated* with the learner's personal, social and
     occupational domains of life.

Within this wider educational perspective, a series of case
studies were undertaken in collaboration with field workers from
various countries. The concrete experiences thus gathered from
different regions, provided valuable insights in identifying
and categorizing possible learning strategies and techniques.
These studies also proved helpful in understanding the scope as
well as limitations of different approaches and programmes and
considering pre-conditions and possible obstacles to be kept in
view in designing and implementing appropriate learning strategies. In order to disseminate as quickly as possible the research findings and related information, a series of international and regional orientation seminars were organized. These
research-based orientation programmes were held for key personnel working directly in this field at the national level and
having the responsibility of developing and implementing programmes of literacy, post-literacy and continuing education in
their own countries. The case study authors were involved as
resource persons in these orientation seminars and their draft
reports used as basic learning materials. The case studies, revised after feedback from the orientation seminars, are now
being published in a UIE series on Post-literacy Studies, for
wider dissemination among policy-makers, practitioners and researchers involved in this field.

The first volume in the series, presents a broad synthesis of different case studies as well as contributions made in various forms by the participants and faculty members of the international and regional orientation seminars conducted in the framework of UIE's integrated project of research and research-based training. In addition, it includes two international approach papers prepared by two eminent specialists, Mr Anil Bordia and Professor Harbans S. Bhola, members of the international research network set up in the initial phase of this project. The subsequent volumes contain national case studies. The present volume, the sixth in the series, presents case studies from the Arab Region namely from Algeria, Egypt and Kuwait. We are grateful to their authors, Mr. Abdellatif Fetni (Algeria), Mr Abdel Fattah Galal and Sami Nassar (Egypt), and Yacoub A. Al-Sharah and Deeb A. Khabbas (Kuwait). We are also grateful to their respective organisations and institutions which extended active cooperation to UIE through their specialists. To all other researchers who prepared case studies as well as to all participants of different seminars, we are extremely thankful.

Our special thanks are due to the Ministry of Culture and Social Services, Government of Kenya; to the Ministry of Education and Culture, Government of India; and to the Ministry of Education, Government of Venezuela; and to their respective National Commissions for Unesco not only for hosting the regional orientation seminars but also for providing support to these programmes in many ways. Likewise, we have enjoyed working with the dynamic local organizational teams set up by our co-ordinators Mr. David Macharia in Kenya, Mr. D.V. Sharma in India and Professor Antonio Valbuena Paz in Venezuela, and we wish to record our deep sense of appreciation and gratitude for their valuable co-operation.

Without the generous extra-budgetary support received by the Institue from the Federal Republic of Germany through the German Commission for Unesco, Bonn this project, involving many researchers and participants from a large number of developing countries in different parts of the world would not have been possible. We are deeply indebted to the Federal German Government and the German Commission for Unesco (DUK) for supporting this important project. Dr.Hans Meinel, Secretary-General of the DUK took personal interest in this endeavour and provided active support and help right from the beginning of this project. Dr Hans-Wolf Rissom from the DUK took an active part in various aspects of the project, and made a valuable contribution.

Ms Judith Schwefringhaus also extended help in the organizational
and other aspects of both research and orientation programmes.
Dr Gisela Steffens from DUK, who replaced Dr Rissom early in
1985, took great interest in the project and contributed much
to its further development. Dr Traugott Schöfthaler who replaced
Dr Steffens in 1986 not only continued cooperation and support
but further intensified it for the enhancement of the project.
In the initial stage of the project, the UIE received support
from the German Foundation for International Development (DSE).
In this respect, the participation and co-operation of Dr Josef
Müller was very much appreciated.

We express our gratitude to the State of Kuwait: to the
Ministry of Education; to the National Commission for Unesco;
to Mr Mohamed Al-Sane, Director of the Gulf Arab States Educational Research Centre and to Dr Yacoub A. Al-Sharah, from the
Ministry of Education for providing UIE with substantial extra-
budgetary support which was used for translating all the documents into Arabic and also for covering the cost of the simul-
taneous interpretation during the Orientation Seminar.

We also received valuable co-operation and guidance from
Unesco Headquarters. Mr Paul Mhaiki and Dr John Ryan from the
Division of Primary Education, Literacy and Adult Education,
and Education in Rural Areas (ED/PLA) provided consultation and
co-operation in planning and implementing various phases of the
project. Dr. Ryan helped us in conducting an international orientation seminar and a regional seminar for Latin America and
the Caribbean, while Mr. Camillo Bonani, Mr Jong Gyu Kim and
Dr. Arthur Gillete from the same Division helped in conducting
the Pan-African, Asian and Arab orientation seminars, respectively. Similarly, Mr B. Haidara and Mr. Tai Afrik from the
Unesco Office for Education in Africa (BREDA), Mr Raja Roy Singh
and Mr. T.M. Sakya from the Unesco Regional Office for Education
in Asia and the Pacific (ROEAP) extended their co-operation in
planning and conducting the African and Asian seminars respectively. For the Orientation Seminar conducted in the Latin American and Caribbean region we received co-operation from Dra.
María E. Dengo de Vargas from the Unesco Regional Co-ordination
Office, Caracas, Drs. S. Romero Lozano, Donald Lemke and José
Rivero, from the Unesco Regional Office for Education in Latin
America and the Caribbean (OREALC). From the Unesco Regional
Office for Education in the Arab States (UNEDBAS) co-operation
was extended by Abdulgadir Yousuf, Director and Abdel Wahid
Yousif, Regional Adviser, in conducting the Orientation Seminar
for the Arab States. We are grateful to all of them.

xviii

From UIE, Dr Adama Ouane and Mr A.M. Ranaweera worked inten-
sively on this project. Dr. Lekh Nath Belbase and Ms Mercy Abreu
de Armengol, who were involved in its Asian and Latin American
phases respectively, also helped to organize and conduct the
programme for the Arab States. The present study was translated
from Arabic under the supervision of Dr. Nabil Salame.
Mr Michael Green and Dr Frederick Gardiner helped in editing
the manuscript. Ms. W. Tränkler took the responsibility of
typing the manuscript for publication. Our thanks are due to all
of them for their valuable work. It is not possible to name all
the colleagues from the UIE who contributed substantially and
in different ways. I wish to express my deep sense of appreciation for their active co-operation right from the inception of
the Project.

It is hoped that the experience of different countries in
the field of post-literacy and continuing education presented
in the synthesis volume as well as other volumes presenting
national case studies in the series will be of use to the policy-makers and practitioners involved in this vital aspect of
education in developing countries.

Ravindra H Dave
Director
Unesco Institute for Education

Chapter 1

LITERACY AND POST-LITERACY
IN THE FRAMEWORK OF CONTINUING EDUCATION:
THE ALGERIAN EXPERIENCE

by

Abdullatif Fetni

1. INTRODUCTION

Algeria's main concern is the promotion and development of human resources. This is an old tradition born during periods of long struggle. Whether living in villages, cities or the desert, the Algerian people derive their strength and ability to make sacrifices from simple faith and determination.

The French Colonial regime, installed in Algeria in 1830 and brought to an end in 1962 after the eight-year war of liberation, left behind an educational legacy which had been devised to acculturate and depersonalize the country, thereby denying the Algerians their history, language, culture and individuality. Koranic precepts and Arabo-Islamic culture have given the people the framework to express their resistance to the assimilative colonial policies and educational system.

The concept of continuing education, which is new for some, is an ancient Islamic concept of education regarded as a fundamental element in opening new horizons of knowledge for the will of man and society in spite of the various ordeals.

Therefore, the education sector is the subject of great concern, which increased during the November revolution. This concern was unanimously demonstrated in every text, charter, major article and decree in the Charter of Tripoli (June 1962):

"The question of culture in our country requires an expansion in the methods of popular education and the mobilisation of all national organizations to combat illiteracy and teach reading and writing to every citizen as soon as possible."

This study is a contribution to the project of the Unesco Institute for Education in Hamburg in co-operation with the German Commission for Unesco, Bonn. The project aims at developing educational strategies for the post-literacy training and continuing education programmes.

2.   BACKGROUND AND CONTEXT

2.1   Geography

Algeria lies in the centre of the Maghreb countries, bordered by the Mediterranean Sea to the north and black Africa to the south. With a surface of 2,381,741 square kilometres, Algeria is the second largest country in Africa after the Sudan, as well as being the largest Arab/Islamic country. Since the administrative partition of 1984, Algeria now includes 48 provinces.

A look at the natural map of Algeria shows that it consists of three distinct large regions, namely the vital upland region, the pastoral mountainous region and the desert region, which is poor in agriculture but rich in combustibles.

The upland region has a relatively mild climate with rain. Economic and demographic activities are concentrated in this region which has many cities.

The mountainous region has a cold climate with little rain. Pastoral life is concentrated in this area, while population density decreases.

The desert region is large with a dry climate which is very hot during the daytime. The Algerian desert is the largest in the world and has a very low population.

2.2   Population

The 1985 census in Algeria estimated a population of 22.5 million, of which one million have emigrated. Average population growth is estimated at 3.2% per year.

The population is expected to reach 25.4 million persons by the end of the second five-year plan and is also expected to reach 34.5 million by the end of the century.

The number of children currently of school age (6-14 years old) is estimated at 820,000. Studies indicate that the group below 45 years of age will represent one-third of the whole population before the end of this decade.

There is no doubt that the demographic development is the concern of many officials and organizers who had to take necessary measures to handle the situation, such as the family planning project, fighting illiteracy and raising the cultural level of women, who are active participants in everyday life.

2.3   Economic Trends

The authorities have made food self-sufficiency a goal and the agricultural sector is regarded as the most important in the present plan. The industrial production is directed at providing the needs of local consumption with the aim of offering a decent life to all citizens.

2.4   The General Situation at the Dawn of Independence

After 132 years of occupation, illiteracy was widespread in cities and villages, among children and adults, even though the colonisers pretend that education was propagated during that period.

Following independence, the Algerian economy was in a depressed state. The fact that much of the country's wealth had been exported to France during the colonial years brought about a situation in which unemployment was widespread, and the opportunities that existed for work were very limited.

Algeria faced the challenge by starting a building and construction campaign on the economic, social and cultural fronts as stipulated in the Charter of 1976:

"... The role of a socialist state is not only limited to changing the relations of productivity but to encouraging maximum development of production capacities which is the material basis of socialism. Within this framework, the state constantly multiplies the material production, assures the social and cultural progress, generalizes education, guarantees health care for every citizen and sees to the well-being of the society. Therefore, it is the duty of a socialist state to reinforce the agricultural, industrial and cultural revolution defined as the basic mission of the socialist structure." (p. 76)

The general efforts exerted in order to fulfill the Charter are noteworthy and conform to the principle of discussing in a democratic manner all the ideas presented, with the aim of adapting theories to the new reality and to taking an objective view of the future.

The spirit of defiance which is a characteristic of revolutionary Algeria is evident in the refusal to accept the abnormal situation imposed by difficult conditions in this part of the world. The Algerian people have struggled for a long time, and continue to do so, to establish themselves among nations. As cited in the Charter, the fight for justice and dignity is a deeply rooted tradition which must be carried on by each economic, social and cultural institution compelled to apply the comprehensive interior development policy by opening new horizons for workers who wish to increase their knowledge, improve their vocational qualifications and obtain necessary certificates.

Interior development represents an important pivot for the implementation of the policy of training programmes for the public and is an active and important contribution to fighting illiteracy. It may call on the assistance of the university and training institutes in the country (p. 269 of the Charter).

2.5   Educational System

The "Algerian Educational Programme and Its Organization" issued in May 1976 under Decree No. 76 reads:

"... the nationalist nature of the education treatise requires that education be in Arabic and should propagate the authentic spiritual and cultural values in order to revive an ancient tradition which is rich and progressive.

Its adaptation depends on the circumstances of the people not only for the abundance of its content but also for its structures, because a national revolution or education revolution can only be realised within the national

structures. A national education programme must, nevertheless, take into consideration the country's interests
concerning its international activities. Therefore, in
the first place an awareness of Arab solidarity is necessary, to be followed by unity with the international
forces fighting for freedom and progress, rejecting international leadership and attempting to realise a new
form of economic and political relationship based simul-
taneously on justice and equality."

The *principles* may be summarized as follows:

- Create a balanced society with the integration of every
  citizen and his participation in progress.

- Provide training for the individual and liberate him
  from all forms of exploitation and subordination.

- Honor and uphold national tradition.

- Encourage science and technology in order to face the
  demands of development and the challenges of civilisa-
  tion.

- Consider education and the acquisition of knowledge as
  the right of every citizen. It is the state's duty to
  provide this right to everyone, regardless of age and
  regional location. The objective is to strive for
  social justice and to create an educated society in
  which each individual assumes his role as a citizen
  conscious of the requirements of his epoch and people.

- Provide education for women to enable them to assume a
  constructive role in society. Women are the primary
  source from whom each individual receives the initial
  education.

The principles are accompanied by a number of *instruc-
tions,* of which the following are the main ones:

- Extend the years of compulsory studies by generalizing
  primary education with its different channels to nine
  years.

- Link the educational content to social and economic
  developments and consider the environment with all its

realities a basic source for education.

- The Arabic language must be the language for education in order to revive and develop it as a living language.

- Instill religious and cultural values in the youth as a basis for forming the citizen and reinforcing his national and religious consciousness.

- Concentrate on practical technological education allowing educated people to implement the acquired knowledge and understand the components of the environment and their influence on it. This type of education imparts a respect for work to young people and encourages them to practice it. Thus, a disdain for manual labour is removed, as is the artificial barrier between the theoretical and practical work, thereby taking up the slack in manual skills and industries.

- Provide vocational training as an extension of primary education (after nine years) and provide a network of centres available to graduates of compulsory education. The concerned ministries are to contribute to its planning and financing.

- Link the education policy to areas of work. This requires a change in educational content in order to obtain the necessary knowledge and skills of modern man.

- Renew the secondary education system and in particular develop the guidance system, diversify the branches and the progress of technical training, as well as public education in the curriculum. Scientific education is to be considered a basic part of the curriculum. Include specialized knowledge with a political, religious and cultural orientation.

- Dedicate efforts to the major operation of organizing adult education by revamping its concept and content within the strategy of comprehensive primary education, encompassing all underprivileged groups of people.

- Give practical meaning to experimental education and field research by organizing comprehensive education research whose function would be to estimate results, follow up the implementation of the plans, supervise

educational performance and develop the curriculum and
methods of education.

- Organize the teaching of foreign languages, which help
  make use of the experience of others, and define its
  role within the framework of our scientific interests
  and economic guidance.

- Provide education for the handicapped, who require
  special considerations and suitable educational facilities.

This system got underway in 1980 by implementing and
generalizing primary education, which is the backbone of this
system. It was carried out according to a well co-ordinated and
gradual plan, which was extended to every part of the country
beginning with the 1985/86 academic year.

This education system is noteworthy in that it is unified
and comprehensive. It integrates the scientific and cultural
dimensions and relates the past to the present and the intel-
lect to manual work in compliance with the development objectives.

Primary education has created a permanent organizational
unit from the first through the ninth year. This organizational
unit includes three consecutive stages in one institution or in
complementary institutions. A number of psychological, biologi-
cal and educational considerations were made in defining the
stages, which are related to the development of a child and its
level of understanding and its motor skills.

First stage: Includes first through third year for children between the ages of six and nine years old. The curriculum is designed to provide manual work with education
and training tools which develop children's motor skills
and help them understand and adapt to the environment.

Second stage: Includes fourth through sixth year for
children between nine and twelve years old. The curriculum is geared to reinforce skills acquired during the
first stage and to continue learning in language, mathematics, environment, and religious and national studies.

Third stage: Includes seventh to ninth year for children
between twelve and fifteen or sixteen years old. The cur-

riculum is dedicated to linguistic, social, cultural, religious and scientific education as well as mathematics, physics and the various sciences of applied technology.

Through its integral curriculum, primary education attempts to offer learners two foreign languages. The first language is introduced in the fourth year and the second in the eighth year, with the aim of enabling learners to benefit from external experiences and contemporary cultures.

The acknowledged method of teaching and education is the stimulation of pupils to practice, research, observe and discover, as well as depend on themselves in acquiring knowledge and accomplishing their work.

The Post-primary Stage of Education

This includes secondary education of both general and vocational types and several institutions of higher education. By the end of primary education, pupils are faced with two alternatives, viz. either to continue their education or prepare themselves for work:

- Secondary education and its various types

- Vocational education and its branches and different levels.

Pupils are guided to one or the other alternative. Their placement depends upon their aptitude on the one hand and the requirements of the country on the other. The interest in this respect is directed towards the re-organization of post-primary education in order to be in harmony with what both precedes and follows it, to correspond with practical life and to adapt to higher education.

Beginning with the 1985/86 academic year, a new organizational form will be set up to deal with the negative aspects of the present system in order to create a balance between public education and vocational education, to remove the barriers between them and to expand the field of applied education and its progress within the different branches of education. In order to cover the different tendencies and dispositions on the one hand and to respond to the demands of development on the other, these branches should vary more.

This new reform necessitates the arrangement of lessons during the first year of secondary education in the form of combined core programmes to lead pupils to find different suitable specializations by the end of this year. They would also find a flexible system facilitating the guidance and distribution process. Bridges should be established between homogenous branches affiliated to one core programme in order to facilitate the process of guidance and, in case pupils face certain difficulties, a change of branch and readaptation.

Vocational Education

The expansion in the fields of vocational education and the diversification of its branches are necessary for the integration of the efforts exerted at the stage of post-primary education, for it must be available to the large number of students who have ended primary education and are not qualified by disposition or grades to continue secondary education in its different branches.

Therefore, vocational education is a specialized short-term educational system related to the fields of work and prepares the student for immediate employment. It provides different sectors with a qualified labour force necessary for the country in facing industrialization and comprehensive development.

Higher Education

The guidance and placement of pupils in the different channels which lead to higher education or where work is carried out are based on the principles of reform, while taking into consideration the requirements of development and university planning in training staff.

It seems necessary to encourage a high rate of learners to enter vocational specializations and exact sciences and to guide the rest towards experimental and human sciences. These judgements are based on the requirements of the country in developing industry, agriculture and the administration, as well as a desire to form distinguished individuals proud of their cultural heritage, their attempts to change their reality, and their contributions to their country.

Table 1

Number of Students in the Educational
and Training System

	1983/84	1984/85	Increase	Rate %
	1	2	3 = 1 + 2	
Primary education	4 810 056	5 183 000	372 944	7.8
Secondary education	325 179	775 000	449 821	138.3
Higher education	104 000	173 000	69 000	66.3
Vocational training	140 000	215 000	75 000	53.6
Apprentice-ship	43 000	100 000	57 000	132.5
Total	5 422 235	6 446 000	1 023 765	18.8

The rate of female participation in primary schools has increased, reaching 42.6% for the two first stages and 40.7% for the third stage. As for secondary education, 5.6 points were added at a rate of 40.4%. Presently efforts are being exerted in order to end the differences in the male and female enrolment rates in the primary schools, which reached 80.6% at the national level.

The rate of enrolment in schools has noticeably increased as a result of the policy of educational democracy. The period of independence has been characterized by the spreading of schools throughout most of the country; the number of national establishments (primary and secondary schools and institutes of technology) has reached 13,000, These establishments enrol approximately 5.5 million pupils, with more than 300,000 teachers, professors, and various staff and administrative employees. In comparing the figures before and after independence, a very large difference is noticeable.

The present situation is distinguished by the unification of education in form and content during the nine years of primary-level education. This involves the structure of the programmes, their coherence and integration, as well as the educational curriculum, which includes scientific, mathematic and vocational subjects.

This unification will encompass the secondary education stage, starting with the 1988/89 academic year. Thus, the Algerian school system has been created on a national basis offering comprehensive education and numerous skills, is open to the environment, and acts with and re-acts to it.

Arabisation

The educational system of the French colonial era developed as in France, reflecting the desire of the administration to assimilate the indigenous population by having French as the vehicular language within the country.

The programme of Arabisation or the use of Arabic as the general language is being implemented by restoring this language in all fields of work and research.

Since Algerian independence, the national authorities have progressively included the Arabic language in compulsory education as well as teaching it to all adult employees of all administrations, organizations, companies and establishments. This is in strong reaction to the colonialist administration, which considered Arabic a dead language and excluded it completely. This programme is aimed at enabling citizens educated in the foreign language to learn their national language and train them to use it professionally. Therefore each organization has created an Arabisation department assigned to plan lessons, appoint teachers, evaluate their work and so forth.

A Higher Council for the National Language was created in order to supervise, co-ordinate and evaluated this national Arabisation operation. A programme was instituted by the council for the whole Republic, and the Arabic language has progressively occupied its natural position in administrative, vocational and industrial activities. Arabisation does not fight other languages but simply

restores the right of every citizen to speak his or her
native language and offers each person the opportunity to
contribute to development and to perform his or her national duty.

A discussion of Arabisation leads to a discussion of the
Algerisation of frameworks. A plan was adopted for the
Algerisation of all the frameworks and curriculum so to
Arabicise the subjects according to the comprehensive
development process of the country. Algerisation, which
is presupposed by Algerians in teaching, raises a few
questions, which have been clarified in the cultural and
educational co-operation obtained from all friendly countries.

Since Algeria differs from other developing countries
with respect to the extent of the deprivation of its population in using their language in acquiring an education
or even in practicing their rights, the popular political
leadership has resorted to the assistance of friends and
sister countries to temporarily assume the function of
teaching. This form of co-operation is quite unique in
the world in both quality and quantity. Algeria has
placed teachers of almost fifty nationalities in the
various schools, as well as having endeavoured to train
Algerians for this purpose. The restoration of the national language has been as difficult as obtaining independence.

3.   LITERACY AND ADULT EDUCATION

3.1   Prior to Independence

The colonial era in Algeria may be said to be marked by
the resistance of the Algerian people on two fronts: firstly,
in the political sphere, where organized resistance starting
with Emir Abd El-Kader culminated in the onset of the eight-
year war of independence; secondly, in the cultural sphere,
where the hitherto neglected Arabic language was taken up in
the fight to overcome the massive problem of illiteracy. Indeed, the National Liberation Front saw this problem as being,
alongside the existence of the colonial regime, a major obstacle to the achievement of true political, economic and cultural independence for the Algerian people.

3.2   Following Independence

At the dawn of independence the officials instituted the
initial measures to be taken in the literacy education of large
groups by opening schools and appointing many teachers to combat the illiteracy left by the occupants.

   a   First stage (1965-1969)

      This stage was the spontaneous confrontation resulting
      from the profound feeling of danger concerning illit-
      eracy. Therefore a major nationwide educational cam-
      paign was organized in all of Algeria for both children
      and adults. Teachers were scarce and those instructing
      in primary schools were compelled to give two hours of
      their time for adult education in all schools.

      During the same period (two years following independ-
      ence), the National Centre for Literacy Education was
      also created in August 1964. According to the Founda-
      tion's decree, the second article assigned to the Cen-

tre stated that "... literacy education was to be carried out in a scientific manner guaranteeing culture to every citizen and so enabling each to contribute to the economic and social development in as short a period of time as possible".

The Centre was also assigned the responsibility of supervising the educational activities undertaken by the local centres, in addition to the educational methods, training necessary staff and estimating the activities at the national level (Article 4 in the Foundation decree).

Article 6 of the same decree affirms "that literacy education is a collective work since it is related to the continuous civil, educational and vocational training of adults".

Achievement and Problems of the First Stage:

While this stage got off to a promising start, enthusiasm soon waned, without leaving behind an administration or organization, programmes or methods.

b   Second stage (1965-1969)

This was the preliminary and preparatory stage for entering the planning period. During that period Algeria witnessed two important developments. One of these was the functional literacy project (Algeria II) financed by UNDP (United National Development Programme) and implemented by UNESCO in the three following regions:

- The agricultural region of Staoueli

- The industrial region of Arzew

- The industrial-agricultural region of Annaba.

The literacy of 100,000 workers in these regions was the project's objective. However, since the beginning of the project in 1967 until February 1974 - eight years after the first stage and three years after the 1971 modifications - only 39,912 workers in the agricultural sector and 13,954 workers in the industrial sector achieved literacy, totalling 53,866 workers, or little more than 50% of the expected results.

The second development was the Three-Year Plan (1967-1969), which was considered as an introduction to and preparation for the First and Second Four-Year Plan, which did not include the literacy problem in their programmes.

Achievements and Problems of the Second Stage

The evaluation made by UNESCO in the book "Estimation of the International Experimental Literacy Programme" issued in 1976, as well as the evaluation made by the National Centre for Literacy Education, is incomplete and the statistics are not detailed. A few probing studies were undertaken on 600 workers who had completed the first educational stage and 350 workers who had completed the second stage in order to ascertain their level of education. Precise statistics are difficult to provide since the evidence remains unusable

This experiment met with many problems, including a lack of co-ordination between the different ministries concerned and the disagreement between Algerian officials and certain UNESCO experts over the basic properties of the project. UNESCO experts wanted to apply the experiment on a limited scale involving the three above-mentioned regions while Algerian officials wanted to expand it and introduce it on the popular literacy scale in view of the large development projects undertaken by the country.

Another problem was the lack of conviction of the concerned ministries regarding the utility of functional literacy on the one hand and the limited human educational and financial resources for this project on the other. Moreover, the lack of supervision, follow-up and animation, in addition to weak national and international efforts and the poor educational level of animators who received only brief training, exacerbated the problem. Finally, the results of the experiment on workers remain unknown as does the impact on their skills, behaviour and productivity.

c Third stage (1970-1977)

This stage included the two four-year plans (1970-1973 and 1974-1977). For the first time since Independence literacy education defined its objectives, set its programmes, prepared the method of instruction, defined a legislation and observed a budget.

The objectives of the first four-year plan involved the literacy of one million citizens on the popular scale and 100,000 workers on the functional scale. The decree of May 1969 assigned the National Centre for General-ised Education the task of propagating education by correspondence, radio and television. This involved 630,000 citizens in an integration of efforts, and of implementing continuing education to meet the requirements of the industrial, agricultural and cultural revolution.

Achievements of the Third Stage

- Within the framework of the first four-year plan literacy for the following number of persons was achieved:

  74,313 in the functional sector out of 100,000, representing 74.3%;

  245,931 in the popular sector out of 1,000,000, representing 24.5%;

  320,244 = the total out of 1,100,000, representing less than one third.

- Within the framework of the second four-year plan, literacy for the following number of persons was achieved:

  131,918 in the functional sector out of 160,000, representing 82%;

  97,870 in the popular sector out of 400,000, representing one quarter;

  229,788 = the total out of 560,000, representing less than one half.

Problems of the Third Stage

- The indifference of the concerned departments towards literacy education

- Considering illiteracy as a marginal problem

- The oppression of bureaucracy over the administrations assigned to this operation

- A continual and arbitrary lack of co-operation in the districts, provinces and popular organizations

- Delays in paying the salaries of animators

- Placing the burden of salaries on the National Centre for Literacy Education when it is not its responsibility

- The interrupted support of the media (radio, television, press)

- The problem of literacy education not being regarded as having economic, cultural and political dimensions

- Campaigns organized only on International Literacy Day or for other celebrations

- Total lack of planning for the expenses of the operation

- No supervision or evaluation of operations at the national level

- No co-ordination between concerned departments

- Animators were too young and ill-trained

- Participating teachers were too few and overworked

- Lack of financial and material resources and equipment

- Lack of participation among the vital capacities in literacy education

- Total lack of any form of stimulation or encouragement to convince adults of the importance of literacy education

- Non-implementation of the articles of the foundation decree of the National Literacy Centre with respect to national and local committees, the creation of local centres and the appointment of inspectors and advisors in every province to supervise literacy education

- Lack of proportion between the construction of the National Literacy Centre and its national function

- Non-contribution by university and research centres of studies concerning literacy and adult education.

The intense legislative movement of the seventies aimed at organizing the education and training process in the different fields of the public sector, introducing the Arabic language in the administrative circles and legally asserting the concept of continuing education in productive agricultural and industrial sectors.

The positive aspects are summarized as follows:

- A firm political determination since independence

- The beginning of legislation on a sound basis

- The foundation decree for the National Literacy Centre in 1964

- The decree for the foundation of the National Centre for the Generalization of Education in 1969

- The decree to link employment and promotion on the administrative scale in obtaining a certificate of the national language in April 1968

- The socialist charter and law for the establishments (Decree 71/74 of November 1971)

- Organization law of prisons and re-education (Decree 72/2 of February 1972)

- Charter of the Agricultural Revolution (Decree 71/73 of November 1971)

- Law for the Councils of Districts and Provinces

- Educational reform (April 1976)

- National Charter and Constitution of 1976

- Law for public work (August 1978).

Every text includes the necessity for education, literacy and continuing education.

d Fourth stage (1978-1985)

This stage was distinguished by the results obtained in literacy and continuing education, which should be reviewed when ascertaining plans for authorisation and approval in order to promote work which will benefit from past experience. Since 1980 all efforts were made to firmly establish primary schools. The Ministry of Education took advantage of this opportunity through the National Literacy Centre to enrich, under the protection of the party, the national political file for literacy education. During the fourteenth ordinary session held on April 28-19, 1985 by the Central Committee of the National Liberation Front, it agreed upon a decree considered as a new specific regulation for work in literacy and continuing education, including the following points:

"The Central Committee adopts the report which includes the policy of literacy and continuing education regarded as an important document of reference.

It calls for the reinforcement and development, as soon as possible, of all the buildings and structures alloted to literacy and continuing education, to facilitate the integration between it and its ability to end illiteracy and to develop and ensure continuing education in the shortest period of time.

The Central Committee calls for the creation of a national organization under the party's supervision for the follow-up, guidance, co-ordination and animation of literacy and continuing education."

According to the results of the former plans, and the Central Committee's agreement on the national policy for literacy education conforming to the principles of the November Revolution, the rate of illiteracy was expected to be as follows:

	1971	1976	1981
Rate of illiteracy among the population aged 10 years and over	67%	56%	48%

The expectations were confirmed by the field study, which arrived at the following rates:

1977: 57.7%
1982: 47.2%

The rate of illiteracy is steadily decreasing as a result of all the efforts exerted, particularly in school education.

However, the efforts should not conceal the dangers of the problem since the total number of illiterates is constantly increasing as indicated in the following table:

Table 2

Illiteracy 1962-1982

Year	Number of illiterates	Total population	Rate of illiteracy
1962	5 600 000	9 000 000	85.0%
1966	5 885 000	12 000 000	75.0%
1977	6 214 000	18 000 000	57.7%
1982	6 341 524	20 000 000	47.2%

The demographic development, in addition to other factors such as poor absorption in schools in remote areas and drop outs, accounts for these results. Drop outs from the fourth grade of primary education are known to relapse into illiteracy. The mean rate of illiteracy in 1982 reached 47.2% (60.18% for women and 34.59% for men).

In spite of the efforts exerted for school education, it is noteworthy that a considerable number of young people still suffer from illiteracy as indicated in the following table:

Table 3

Illiteracy by Age Groups

Age group	1977	1982
15-17	39.7%	20.4%
18-59	68.3%	51.6%
60 and above	92.0%	90.7%

On the other hand, the rate of illiteracy among workers is 51.6%. Illiteracy results in a poor standard of production which hinders development.

4. LITERACY PROGRAMMES AND CONTINUING EDUCATION

4.1 The Project Presented during the Fourth Conference of the National Liberation Front Party

The project defined the following strategies for literacy and continuing education:

"Set a national programme for literacy education capable of mobilising all the necessary human and material resources in order to radically put an end to illiteracy in the sectors of production, services, co-operatives and socialist villages."

The report on literacy and continuing education ratified by the Central Committee of the National Liberation Front during its fourth session in 1985 stipulated the following:

"A study on the problems of literacy and continuing education for adults aims at placing this programme within a comprehensive strategy for public education and assimilating it within an economic and social development plan."

Continuing education has two closely related elements: literacy and adult education.

The concept of continuing education should not be viewed as only representing adult education nor should illiteracy be considered as a problem isolated from education, but as the backbone of continuing education.

Therefore, a comprehensive study of the concept of continuing education is necessary for an integrated educational system adapted both to individuals and to the demands of a society facing rapid scientific and technological development, as well as economic and social demands.

Ensuring lifetime education widens the scope for continuing education and any necessary vocational re-education. Thus all the methods of education should be developed and adapted.

Continuing education, therefore, should not be viewed from a narrow perspective as though it were a simple vocational training, for it actually aims at ensuring scientific knowledge, better control over daily vocational matters and guaranties greater earning power. The ultimate aim of this education is the continuing work of human progress in every field.

Continuing education, which includes all age groups, involves the different activities which respond to the demands of social development and is therefore important and necessary to every developing society desirous of retaining its position among nations undergoing continual transformations in different fields.

The literacy process included in the comprehensive operation of continuing education cannot be limited to simple programmes unrelated to the environment or the existing educational systems and training programmes, but should be viewed as a system receiving the same importance as the national education programme.

4.2   The National Centre for Literacy Education

The National Centre for Literacy Education was created in August 1964 under the supervision of the Ministry of National Guidance. Work, however, only began two years after its creation, in 1966, when it became an independent public establishment with a special budget according to Decrees Nos. 61-66.

A board of directors supervises the progress of this establishment under the chairmanship of the Secretary General of the Ministry of Education. Its main concerns are the following:

- The Management of the Centre and administration of its laws, budget and financial accounts;

- Carrying out dialogues on the issues raised by the Minister of National Education.

A director is appointed by decree issued by the President

of the Republic, according to a proposal submitted by the Minister of National Education, to manage the Centre. The director is assisted in his functions by inspectors, professors, teachers and technicians.

Representatives of the centres in the provinces animate field work at the local level.

The present tendency is to give new impetus to literacy education and continuing education as stipulated in the National Political Project for Literacy and Continuing Education:

"The Central Committee is invited to create a national organization under the supervision of the party to follow-up, supervise, guide, co-ordinate and animate literacy and continuing education."

The Centre attempts to control its departments and define the working methods adapted in the critical stage of the comprehensive development plan undertaken by the country. Work is distributed to the Communication and Information Department, Research, Training and Formation Department, Department for the Production of Adult Education Methods, Programming and Estimation Department and the Department for Financial Administration. The Centre has branches in all the provinces of the Republic.

The adopted method in the Centre aims at activating field operations, setting up the appropriate programmes for the intended groups and training field workers. The Centre is sensitive to the learners' desires and attempts to evaluate them so as to contribute to development.

4.3   Methodology Adopted in Setting Up Programmes

In setting up programmes for literacy and continuing education, the requirements and capacities of learners as well as national considerations must be evaluated, since the value of the education offered to learners depends on the extent of benefit they receive. Many programmes were prepared and presented without any result for they were outside the scope of the learner's reality, such as the teaching of reading which did not correspond to the actual requirements of learners. According to the education principle each individual is entitled to decide what he or she would like to learn, but this principle is seldom respected during implementation.

Those setting up programmes in the National Centre for Literacy Education attempt to realize the following objectives:

- Provide learners with knowledge both fundamental and relative to their lives and widen their scope of culture and awareness.

- Provide learners with the necessary technical and vocational knowledge for their work and reinforce specialization in order to improve his performance standard, their standard, increase their productivity and encourage active participation in society. Motivate the learners to keep pace with the developments and changes which occur in production units.

- Provide learners with the necessary basic skills of reading, writing and arithmetic to enable them to profit from educational and training programmes as well as to augment general knowledge.

- Develop tendencies, inclinations, emotions, values and behaviour.

- Develop the learners' esteem for work as well as their respect for others, opinions and order.

- Facilitate their adaptation to the working environment and to the economic, social and political changes occuring in his society.

Unless literacy and continuing education programmes conform to the requirements and desires of learners and follow the national education objectives, they are incomplete and unacceptable.

We find in evaluating the requirements of adult learners that they have numerous social, religious, economic and political activities, which demand knowledgeable handling. Therefore, learners require communication skills such as reading, writing, counting and an understanding of the meaning of numbers. Moreover, learners are members of society and interact with their peers; therefore they are interested in being informed of news and events that affect their lives.

According to this principle, the literacy and continuing education programmes include the following subjects:

- Reading
- Writing
- Arithmetic.

In the past the traditional and popular literacy programmes were limited to reading, writing and counting. Anima-
ting classes in general culture were neglected and thus the
programmes did not fulfil the required purpose and learners
were not inclined to continue education. Therefore the National
Centre for Literacy Education's introduction of general culture
as an independent subject has been largely appreciated by adult
learners.

The academic subjects are characterized by their integration regardless of the objectives and benefits of each subject
separately.

4.4   Functional Literacy

Functional literacy assists productive individuals in
developing and raising the standard of their capacities and
productivity by providing training and instruction in their
fields of specialization, whether in an industrial or a rural
milieu. It also helps individuals solve their daily problems
and enables them to actively participate in their community.
Thus, functional literacy education is regarded as an integral
part of the stages of development related to the individual's
life, work and society. Literacy education is not a final
objective but a means of obtaining useful knowledge and new
skills which help improve the citizen's quality of life.

Traditional or popular literacy education, which teaches
the principles of reading, writing and counting, is limited and
does not contribute to the formation of good citizens inter-
acting with and conscious of their roles in society.

The National Centre for Literacy Education has therefore
adopted the concept of functional literacy education to provide
learners with a social, economic, political and vocational
education as a complement to the traditional reading, writing
and counting literacy education.

Studies and research in this field have confirmed that
illiteracy and underdevelopment are related and that no country
with a widespread rate of illiteracy can make a great deal of

progress unless this obstacle is overcome. Experiments have proven that ordinary literacy education does not fulfil the requirements and demands of a modern society since it requires quick and comprehensive development in order to enjoy the results of modern industry and an increase in the national income. Therefore it is compelled to import industries and the necessary machines and equipment but encounters the obstacle of incompetent technicians responsible for supervision and operation. Industry is thus faced with the two following alternatives:

- Either it imports technicians from abroad as it did for the machines, which results in a form of subordination

- Or it attempts to train citizens to operate the machines. This is unquestionably the preferred choice since it will help train and find sufficient competent workers for different projects.

Objectives of Functional Literacy

Functional literacy aims at educating and training learners in their field of work, whether industrial or agricultural, by providing them with the expertise necessary to improve their work. Training farmers, for instance, in applying and adopting the right methods of agriculture and the maintenance of different machines as well as training workers in other sectors, leads to economic development.

This form of education aims at building a society of competent men and women who will contribute to technological development and provide the necessary labour force for each sector, ensuring the progress of economic projects.

It also aims at transforming work methods. Workers who once employed methods passed down from their fathers and forefathers are shown how scientific methods can increase productivity.

Finally, functional literacy education aims at promoting development in a worker's habits and behaviour, which should be incorporated in his life and work. In the past workers viewed work solely in terms of salary; when workers are promoted to supervisors, however, work occupies their minds outside working hours as well.

Characteristics of Functional Literacy Education

Functional literacy education is applied in specialized and defined sectors and differs from traditional literacy education in its working method.

It concentrates on production sectors in order to train workers and increase productivity. Its impact on production may be easily perceived. Since most workers are illiterate, functional literacy education has been necessary for these sectors to prevent production obstruction for too long and to assure the necessary skills.

Concept of Functional Literacy Education and Its Development

The country needs qualified citizens who can contribute to development programmes.

Development is concerned with qualitative and quantitative changes in the different aspects of an individual's life and in the life of societies. Whether economic, social, political or cultural, all these aspects interact. Therefore development demands sound qualifications, increase of investment and resources, as well as competent manpower - all of which require sound planning.

In view of the dangerous effects of illiteracy on a developing society, many countries have endeavoured to spread compulsory education in order to counteract one of the sources of illiteracy.

However, the rapid scientific and technological progress has created pressures on these countries, which can no longer count on compulsory education alone to keep pace with the high demand on human and material capacities. Therefore, the inevitable decision was to prepare adult citizens who are actually part of the process of production, in other words the labour force, by educating and training them to understand all the economic and social developments which occur in the country. In turn this awareness will reflect on the productivity and methods of work as well as on the concepts and achievements required by development.

Literacy programmes in the past were concerned with illiterates in general and were traditional in approach. They lacked sound planning in spite of the problems and the expansion and exigencies of the programmes. The UNESCO organization appointed a new method of treating the problems which is the concentrated selectivity method geared to placing the focus of literacy programmes on economic and social development.

Algeria has made use of the international experiments in that field and adapted and modified them to its environment. Among the concepts from which work methods have been derived is the Arab Strategy for Literacy Education undertaken by the National Centre for Literacy Education. This strategy conforms to the belief in Arab nationalism, attempting to achieve a unified view in order to overcome difficulties. So far the principles of a political decision and the people's will - the two basic elements of the strategy - have been realized and the country's highest authorities for national literacy and continuing education policy have adopted the strategy.

The political report includes most of the principles concerned with combatting illiteracy through compulsory fundamental education, its generalization and the implementation of the integration of formal and informal education. Scientific methods have been applied in facing the problem.

4.5   Traditional Literacy Education

This programme was created for those groups of illiterates who do not fit into any specific framework. In the past traditional literacy was limited to teaching reading, writing and arithmetic.

The reading texts of this programme included certain social problems faced daily by the illiterates. The aim of this form of literacy education was to offer learners the possibility of reading letters, newspapers and documents of relevance to them, rather than achieving a comprehensive education. Thus ordinary literacy programmes did not differ much from the programmes of the first stages of primary schools, which are geared towards communication skills, i.e. reading and writing. These programmes disregarded the assimilation of illiterates into their environment, therefore they were revised in order to comply with the objectives of the socialist revolution and follow in the footsteps of functional literacy programmes in method and content.

Algeria's various literacy programmes are divided according to production sectors such as literacy for the industrial sector and literacy for the agricultural sector.

4.6 Teacher Training for Adult Classes

A training course is organized for each group of animators and instructors in order to teach them the methods and forms of instructing adults. The training lasts one month and includes meetings to discuss problems confronted in field work.

The training of teachers for adult courses is necessary in order to understand the psychology of adults and the special methods and forms of teaching. Therefore, teachers in children's schools cannot teach adults unless they attend a training course.

The importance of teachers for literacy and continuing education programmes became a preoccupation for officials in the sector as far as selecting and instructing those teachers. Teachers for adults may be divided into three types as follows:

First Type

Full-time adult instructors, which are the best type of teachers since they acquire the experience and learn all about adult education.

This type of instructor is the keenest in implementing the required methods and employing the necessary systems as well as investing interest. This type of specialization represents the backbone of continuing education.

Second Type

A part-time instructor who has another job other than adult education and holds this function as an extra job or as a volunteer.

Even though these instructors are outside the circle of supervision, cannot be impelled to follow specific educational methods and are not always regular in their attendance, they form an important part which should not be underestimated.

Third Type

This type of instructor is composed of a selection of workers from different sectors who are paid for this work.

They are often poorly qualified in the field of education since they have rarely received any training to teach others. The reasons for resorting to this type of teacher are as follows:

- They belong to the sector, therefore are aware of the problems concerning them

- They are workers, therefore understand the problems of their peers

- They can be commissioned by the sector without requiring a new budget.

5.   LEARNING STRATEGIES FOR POST-LITERACY WITHIN THE
     FRAMEWORK OF CONTINUING EDUCATION

The efforts exerted in adult education are not only
limited to literacy education but also provide opportunities
for learners to join other vocational establishments or to
continue their education. The National Centre for the Generalization of Education was created to continue an educational
system outside schools.

5.1   The National Centre for the Generalization of Education

This Centre was created in May 1969, in accordance with
Decree No. 37-69, "The National Centre for the Generalization
of Education by Correspondence, Radio and Television". It is
a public establishment responsible for external education.

The establishment offers correspondence courses in all
subjects and assists and supports the educational system for
learners who for some reason or other could not complete their
education. The Centre offers courses in vocational and management education.

The correspondence courses are reinforced by radio and
television programmes and specialized instructors who organize
the courses in the centres specially created for that purpose.

A number of branches of this establishment exist in the
provinces and the numbers of affiliated learners are rapidly
growing; its services are attracting activities and renewal.

5.2   Establishments Subordinated to Other Sectors

Education is not limited to the national education sector, even though this is the major function of the Ministry of
Education. Other sectors are also interested in educational

activities, especially the social and economic sectors. Training programmes within the framework of continuing education have been organized in order to improve workers' revenues.

Most of the establishments and economic units numbering more than one hundred workers created a training directorate in accordance with Decree Nos. 214-64, which assure worker training and the improvement of their standard. A number of training courses were organized for all the workers who had not received work training and the co-ordination between establishments under the aegis of the Ministry of National Education, the National Centre for Literacy Education and the National Centre for the Generalization of Education was respected.

Other sectors, such as the Ministry of Vocational Education, have established vocational education programmes through training courses and workshops or by correspondence courses.

5.3   Guidance

Educational establishments for continuing education, whether traditional or specialized, have received a positive response, which results from the comprehensive development programme requiring qualified labour.

Guidance is directed towards illiterates with two principal aims: first, to motivate officials in different sectors to give special attention to this subject, and second, to encourage illiterates to join literacy education programmes. The following methods are used for that purpose:

- Announcements in print and broadcast media

- Articles in newspapers and magazines

- Posters, slogans and other vehicles for propaganda

- Seminars and academic days for guidance and information, organized by the Party and popular institutions.

The creation of a permanent national organization under the supervision of the Party for the follow-up, supervision, guidance, co-ordination and animation of literacy and continuing education is anticipated. The National Policy Decree for

Literacy and Continuing Education (drawn up during the Fourteenth Session of the Central Committee) stipulates the following:

> "The mass media is invited to contribute actively in the endeavours of literacy and continuing education programmes by setting up well-planned programmes on television, radio and in the written press serving the concerned groups and assisting them in their literacy and continuing education according to the decrees made by the political leadership."

6. CONCLUSION

The latest decree of the Central Committee regarding the National Policy for Literacy and Continuing Education mentions the following:

"The Algerian experience in combating illiteracy did not attain the expected objectives as a result of the lack of a clear and integral plan and the absence of a suitable climate for a generalized use of the national language."

The main obstacles in literacy and continuing education were mentioned in the report concerning the literacy policy.

The problem of illiteracy is still very acute in Algeria since half the population outside school falls into this category. The results could have been positive if a national policy had been defined concerning:

- The official departments for guidance, mobilization and co-ordination at both the national and local levels

- The functions of the vocational organization responsible for literacy and continuing education

- The role of mass media and popular organizations in guidance and mobilization

- The participation of all the different sectors such as popular municipal councils, popular organizations and national establishments

- The supervision and follow-up of the different operations at the national level, with periodic evaluations of results, and carrying out the necessary modifications at the right time.

In analysing the results of literacy education in Algeria, we can draw the following conclusions:

- Worldwide experiences have proved the practical impossibility of obtaining a satisfactory standard of literacy education through developing the methods of teaching alone, and even if it were feasible, it would require three or more generations to attain the required results.

  Experiments have proven that adult literacy education encourages children to attend school and decreases the drop-out rate; this reflects on the educational system itself.

  At the strategic level, illiteracy must be fought on two fronts: primary and adult education. By generalizing primary education and adult literacy education, both are reinforced.

- Even though a general consensus exists on the necessity of combatting illiteracy, it is not considered a national problem. A complex problem requires a well-defined and clear cut policy within the national economic and social development plan.

  Implementation implies the commitment of every sector, which therefore requires well-planned co-ordination. The mobilization of all the concerned organizations and establishments are two elements currently missing. Turning literacy education into an administrative vocational skill is bound to fail since it has no popular basis.

Therefore, setting a well-defined policy for literacy education, correctly estimating the situation and defining a practical plan are necessary and urgent.

Algeria, nevertheless, will always surmount difficulties in its development and retain its determination to continue work for literacy and continuing education programmes.

REFERENCES

1) The National Charter

2) Various party decrees

3) The official publication, National Education, a special
   issue including decree nos. 16-35 of April 1976

4) Decree including the national policy for literacy and
   continuing education - Fourteenth session

5) Report on the Policy for Literacy and Continuing Education

6) Second Five-Year Plan (1985-1989).
   General report - January 1985

APPENDIX 1

EDUCATIONAL MATERIALS

a) *Agricultural sector*

Reading books

1 - *We work and Learn on the Farm* part I.
A book for the rural area in general.

2 - *We work and Learn on the Farm* - part II.
A book for the rural area and for follow-up.

3 - *We work and Learn on the Farm.*
A special book for workers in grain-producing
regions.

4 - *We work and Learn in Co-operatives.*
A special book for workers in co-operatives which is
a vocational organism for farmers.

b) *Industrial sector*

Reading books

1 - *We work and Learn* - part I.
For miners.

2 - *We work and Learn* - part II.
For miners (follow-up stage).

3 - *We Work and Learn in Textile Industries* - part I.
For the textile sector.

4 - *We Work and Learn in Textile Industries* - part II.
For textile workers (follow-up stage).

5 - *We Work and Learn*
Special for the food sector (mills and kneading troughs).

6 - *We Work and Learn*
For the construction sector.

7 - *We Work and Learn*
For industrial establishments (joint core programmes).

8 - *We Work and Learn in the Construction Sectors*
For workers in the building sector. Prepared in participation with the Ministry of Building and Construction.

c) Popular sector

1 - *We work and Learn* - part I.
A book for reading training based on matters of interest in the daily social, civil and political life of an Algerian citizen.

2 - *We work and Learn* - part II.
For the follow-up stage. This book offers more advanced texts for the training of reading. This programme depends on the generalization of the national language.

3 - *We Learn Our Language"* - part I.
Trains in the reading of texts on daily social life.

4 - *We Learn Our Language* - part II.
Follow-up and training for advanced reading with some information on grammar.

5 - *We Learn Our Language* - part III.
Follow-up stage. A book of reading and grammar suitable for adults preparing for the primary certificate.

6 - *Work and Learn* - part I.
   Specifically for women.

7 - *Work and Learn* - part II.
   For women (follow-up stage).

8 - *Learn Reading and Writing* - part I.
   Joint core programme for the public sector.

9 - *Learn Reading and Writing* - part II (under print).
   Joint core programme for the public sector
   (follow-up).

APPENDIX 2

COMPLEMENTARY EDUCATIONAL MATERIALS

a) A series of guides

Specially prepared for instructors of literacy and adult education programmes on teaching methods for reading and its progression.

1 - Instructor's Guide for the book *Work and Learn* from the public sector.

2 - Instructor's Guide for training in teaching the principles of Arabic grammar.

3 - Instructor's Guide for the book *We Learn Our Language* with a curriculum of the courses and an explanation of certain chapters.

4 - Instructor's Guide for the book *Work and Learn* for women.

5 - Instructor's Guide for the book *We Work and Learn in Industry*.

6 - Instructor's Guide for the book *We work and Learn on the Farm*.

7 - Instructor's Guide for the book *We Work and Learn* for the mining sector.

8 - Instructor's Guide for the book *We Work and Learn* for the textile sector.

9 - Instructor's Guide for the book *We Work and Learn* for the food sector (mills and kneading throughs).

10 - Instructor's Guide for the book *We work and Learn* for the construction and building sector.

11 - Instructor's Guide for the book *Learn to Read and Write* - joint core programme for the popular sector.

12 - Instructor's Guide for the book *We Work and Learn* for the building materials sector.

13 - Instructor's Guide for the book *We Learn Our Language* - part III.

b) Arithmetic

1 - *Arithmetic Training:* a booklet teaching the four arithmetic operations and the decimal system for daily use.

2 - *Arithmetic Notes:* a booklet of 62 notes inserted according to the programme. It indicates to the instructor the method of progressing in arithmetic lessons.

APPENDIX 3

AUDIO-VISUAL MATERIALS

1 - Film on "Why Literacy Education"

(16 and 35 mm) - The film discusses the problems of illiteracy in Algeria and the world at large, and can be used for guidance.

2 - Film on the Astawaly Experience

(35 mm) - Arabic and French speaking film on the literacy experience in the region of Astawaly undertaken by Algeria with the assistance of UNDP and UNESCO.

3 - Film on "Tree Pruning"

(35 mm) - Arabic speaking film on the scientific methods for pruning trees warning of the dangers of employing unscientific methods.

4 - Film on "Fertilization"

(35 mm) - Arabic speaking film on the methods of fertilizing as well as a guide to the kinds of fertilizers to use.

5 - Film on "The Method of Teaching to Read"

(35 mm) - Arabic speaking film on the method of teaching adults to read and write and the stages necessary for learners to achieve their objectives.

6 - Flashcards

Letter and words in large print on cards to assist instructors and students in understanding what is presented in an simple, easy manner.

7 - Pictures

Pictures from the assigned books enlarged and re-
produced to be placed on the blackboard at the beginning of a lesson to introduce the topic.

8 - Boards

Large boards to indicate the subjects presented and
for deducing the information and proper methods to
be employed in the agricultural, economic and social
fields.

The greater part of the educational material is prepared
and achieved by the National Centre for Literacy Education
which also prints it with its limited resources, in spite of
the limited technical means and the difficulties encountered.
The Centre distributes these methods to interested establishments and ministries at nominal cost decided upon by its Board
of Directors. It still has hope of receiving assistance from
different sectors in the future according to the decree of the
Central Committee during its last session:

"The Central Committee asks that human, material and
financial resources be provided for this operation to
implement a well-planned programme for all the popular
groups."

APPENDIX 4

RESEARCH AND STUDIES

We specially mention:

Research

1 - "A View on Combatting Illiteracy in Algeria"

A report which studies the dangers of illiteracy in Algeria and the different attempts for its eradication, especially the endeavours of the National Centre for Literacy Education.

2 - "The Problem of Illiteracy in Algeria"

This report includes an historical view of illiteracy before and after independence, the different campaigns against illiteracy and finally the international experimental programme for literacy education.

3 - "Combatting Illiteracy and the Efforts Exerted in Algeria

This research includes an explanation on the creation of the National Centre for Literacy Education in Algeria, its functions and its activities.

4 - "The Experiment of Functional Education in Algeria"

A view on functional education in Algeria, its stages and the difficulties encountered.

5 - "The Experiment of Teaching Arabic on Television"

A research on the early experiment on television in 1969, illustrating the aims of these lessons and the method of presentation.

6 - "The National Centre for Literacy Education and Its Endeavours in the Field of Training

This research illustrated the training activities undertaken by the Centre and the weekly debates held by the animators with the programmes prepared for these activities.

Studies

1 - "Illiteracy and Its Dangers"

This study illustrates the problem of illiteracy, its spread and its impact on society and the individual as a means of oppression and imperialism.

2 - "Illiteracy and Workers"

This includes the influence of a worker's illiteracy on his productivity and the necessity of training the worker and disseminating information. The education of workers is considered a very profitable investment.

3 - "The Impact of Illiteracy on Production"

A study illustrating the negative impact illiteracy has on work and production. The skills and education of a worker increases productivity, which indicates the necessity of education.

4 - "Organize Education in the Class"

An explanation on education, its requirements, what is expected to be prepared by the instructor and the method of handling adult learners.

5 - "Discussion"

Adults have previous knowledge which may be employed and supplemented through discussion. This paper illustrates a number of situations faced by the instructor in class.

6 - "Adult Education, Its Objectives and Stages"

An illustration of the different stages of adult education, different concepts and the basic differences between adult and child education.

7 - "The Aims of Functional Literacy Education"

This study includes the concept and aims of functional literacy education.

8 - "Aspects and Methods of Education"

This study was presented to the Preparatory Committee for the creation of the Higher Committee for Literacy Education under the supervision of the party and includes a detailed study on the problems of illiteracy and a few proposed solutions.

9 - "The Ordinary General Programme for Literacy Education"

This programme was set to indicate the stages, subjects and period necessary for literacy education.

10 - "Farming in Algeria"

A view on farming in Algeria, detailing the different crops, farming experiments and cattle rearing which is among the important sources of life and national income of the people.

11 - "Farming in Automated Farms"

Farmers no longer are hired workers but the animators of certain processes of automation.

12 - "Literacy Education and Economic Development"

Political independence alone is insufficient to develop a country. Since economic development requires modern equipment and trained manpower it must be accompanied by worker training and education.

13 - "How to Learn to Read and Write"

The method of teaching is as important as the educational material, therefore this paper illustrates the methods of teaching how to read.

14 - "Arithmetic, Its Aims and Stages"

The method of teaching arithmetic and the objectives of arithmetic education.

15 - "Illiteracy in Algeria in 1982"

A general study regarding illiteracy.

Chapter 2

LEARNING STRATEGIES FOR POST-LITERACY AND BASIC LEVEL EDUCATION IN EGYPT IN THE PERSPECTIVE OF LIFELONG EDUCATION

by

Abdel Fattah Galal
and
Sami Nassar

1. INTRODUCTION

1.1 Lifelong Education according to Islam

"In the name of Allah, the Beneficent, the Merciful.
Read: In the name of thy Lord who createth man from a
clot.
Read: And thy Lord is the Most Bounteous, who teacheth
by the pen.
Teacheth man that which he knew not."
(Surah Al-âlaq: 1-5)

With this verse of the Koran, which descended upon the
prophet Mohamed, came the beginning of the Islamic religion;
therefore the concept of reading, knowledge and education is
directly related to Islam. The search for knowledge became a
fundamental duty of every Muslim. Allah ordained the prophet
to increase his knowledge when saying: "My Lord! increase me
in knowledge." (Surah Tâ Hâ - 114) Certain interpreters said
that the main desire voiced by the prophet was for more knowledge. The prophet, conscious of the importance of knowledge
and education repeated this prayer: "God Almighty, let me
make use of the knowledge Thou givest me, and teach me more,
laudation be to Allah for all His blessings." This prayer is
the orientation for every Muslim to mindfully continue to
learn and acquire knowledge for his own benefit and that of
his nation. All Muslims have an obligation to preserve by
applying the skills and conduct they have acquired.

Lifelong education is an obligation in Islam since
every human being is considered to be born ignorant: "And

Allah brought you forth from the wombs of your mothers knowing
nothing, and gave you hearing and sight and hearts that haply
ye might give thanks." (Surah Al-naāl - 78) With the capacity of
the mind, hearing and sight, every human being is to pursue
knowledge; it is every Muslim's obligation to acquire knowledge
regardless of its source or location, as pointed out by the
prophet when saying: "A word of wisdom is the believer's right
wherever he may receive it;" and if knowledge is accessible
elsewhere and requires travelling then it becomes a duty to
pursue it,as said in the Koran: "Of every troop of them, a
party only should go forth, that they (who are left behind) may
gain sound knowledge in religion, and that they may warn their
folk when they return to them, so that they may beware." (Surah
Al-Tawba 122) The same idea was taught by its prophet when
saying:

> Whoever seeks knowledge, Allah facilitates his path to
> heaven and angels bless and protect them, and all that
> is in the heavens and in the lands as well as the
> whales in the seas beg for His pardon. Holders of knowl-
> edge are at a higher degree than simple believers; as
> the full moon is above the other planets, holders of
> knowledge are also the inheritors of the prophets who
> are the true inheritors of knowledge. Therefore, holders
> of knowledge are the fortunate ones.

Education in Islam is the fundamental condition for holding any position of responsibility or assuming any leading function: "Learn before ruling," says Omar Ibn Khattab in conformity
with: "Allah will exalt those who believe among you, and those
who have knowledge, to high ranks." (Surah Al Mujadilah - 11)
Or: "Seek knowledge from birth until death," as ordained by the
Imam Aly. Knowledge and education are viewed as a divine blessing in Islam. "And We verily gave knowledge unto David and
Solomon, and they said: Praise be to Allah, who hath preferred
us above many of His believing slaves!" (Surah Al-Naml - 15)
Having bestowed the blessing of knowledge upon Moses: "And when
he reached his full strength and was ripe, We gave him wisdom
and knowledge. Thus We reward the good." (Surah Al Qasas - 14)
Those who acquire wisdom have received the greater blessing:
"He giveth wisdom unto whom He will, and he unto whom wisdom is
given, he truly hath received abundant good. But none remember
except men of understanding." (Surah Al-Baqara - 269)

Holders of knowledge leaving behind useful knowledge are
blessed in their afterlives as long as humanity benefits from
such a knowledge, thus says the prophet: "After death man is

detached from all his deeds except for three, continuous alms-
giving, a useful knowledge and a virtuous child who prays for
him."

Seeking and spreading knowledge is the duty of every
individual during his lifetime and leaving behind useful knowledge is blessed in the afterlife.

The first school of adult education was created by the
prophet Mohamed to instruct his disciples. This school was the
first mosque, which he built in Medina with his honourable
friends. The mosques later developed into large universities
spreading to every capital and city of the Islamic world. The
prophet said unto them: "My creator has ordained me to instruct
you of that which you ignore ..." "Allah has not sent me to
coerce you but to teach you gently ..." and this was witnessed
and confirmed by his friends among whom one said: "I have never
met a teacher better than him."

The concept of lifelong education sprang from the early
sources of Islam, was implemented by the first Muslims who created the first humanitarian civilization during the Middle Ages
and was the inspiration for European contemporary civilization.

1.2   Lifelong Education in Egypt

The Azhar University in Egypt conformed to the philosophy
of lifelong education since it allowed students, regardless of
age, to enrol in any field of education, with the freedom to
select the instructor of their choice. The Azhar mosque, as well
as the other large mosques which were transformed into universities, were adopted in Europe as a model for adult education, and
for lifelong education in particular.

Educational institutions for both children and adults
functioned according to the concept of lifelong education
through the 'Kuttab' schools for children and mosques for
adults. Learners move from one mosque to another until they
acquire the educational level for the Azhar University, which
provides learners with higher education and specializations in
various fields, in addition to other educational institutions.

With colonialism in Egypt, the system of education
changed from the above-mentioned system to a reformed system of
three stages of education for the purpose of training govern-

ment functionaries. This disrupted the concept of lifelong education and illiteracy appeared.

Various methods of supressing illiteracy have been attempted in Egypt since the beginning of the twentieth century. Today, the concept of lifelong education is very clear, therefore many attempts are undertaken in formal and nonformal education in addition to the various institutions for adult education.

The present research attempts to illustrate the dimensions of learning strategies for post-literacy education and continuing education in Egypt, along with the efforts contributed by the Unesco Education Institute in Hamburg. It aims at preventing the relapse into illiteracy through the experiences and expertise of the different countries involved, for both adult neo-literates and drop-outs from the primary stage who have already acquired the basic skills of reading and writing.

The research conforms to the principles of the Unesco Institute for Education in opening new horizons and opportunities for both children and adults to continue their education according to the concepts of lifelong education. The present research also conforms to the method proposed by the Unesco Institute for Education, which is designed to compare the strategies of different countries, enabling the world to adopt the appropriate learning strategies with a view to the democracy of education, development and the well-being of humanity.

2. A GENERAL BACKGROUND OF EGYPT

2.1 Location and Population

Egypt is located in the north-eastern corner of Africa and in the heart of the Arab world, as well as at the centre of the ancient world. It is one of the Mediterranean countries and, therefore, since ancient times, has been a recipient of all civilization and religious currents. It has witnessed the birth of the Ancient Pharaonic civilization which then interacted with the Greek and Roman civilizations. The three religions - Judaism, Christianity and Islam - were embraced by Egypt and finally the interaction with modern European civilization took place.

Egypt is bordered to the north by the Mediterranean Sea, to the east by Palestine and the Red Sea, to the south by the Sudan and to the west by Libya. The total area of Egypt, including the desert and its regional waters, is 1,002,000 square kilometres. The four major geographic divisions of Egypt are the Nile valley, the Western desert, the Eastern desert and the Sinai peninsula.

According to the latest demographic survey of 1976, the population totals 37 million (36,626,304) with approximately 43.8% living in urban areas and 56.2% living in rural areas. According to 1982 estimates, the population numbers approximately 45 million.

2.2 Economic Activity

The gross national product of Egypt is US $ 26,400,000

million, and annual per capita income is US $ 690.

Farmers and fishermen account for 47.7% of the labour force; those working in transitional industries account for approximately 13.3%; in service sectors, approximately 18.2%; in the trade, restaurant and hotel sector, 8.4%; in transport, storage and communications, 4.7%; and finally, in construction, 4,1%. The remaining percentage of the population works in different activities.

Approximately 28% of the productive population work in the public sector, and the remaining 72% are employed in the private sector.

The surface area is approximately 238 million feddans, of which the largest part is uncultivated desert land, with the exception of 6.3 millions feddans owned by approximately 2.5 million landowners. Agriculture in Egypt is dependent on water from the Nile, and the government is exerting maximum efforts to demarcate all the sources of underground water in the desert in order to promote agriculture.

Minerals are an important resource in Egypt. Oil is the major resource with a total of 32.9 million tons produced in 1980-1981; as for the production of phosphate, in the same year it was 4,946,000 tons.

There are many industries in Egypt, of which textiles and weaving, iron steel, aluminium, oil refining, food and chemicals are the most important. One of the major sources of income for Egypt is the Suez Canal, in addition to its strategic position.

Economic activity in Egypt is part of the comprehensive development plan stipulated by the People's Assembly and implemented by the Ministry of Planning and International Co-operation.

2.3   Political System

Egypt is a republic divided into executive, legislative and judicial authorities. The political system is based on a multi-party democracy with a permanent constitution stipulating that it is an Arab State, its religion is Islam and the official language is Arabic. The President is elected and is the head of the executive authority for six renewable years. The legislative authority is assumed by the People's Assembly, whereas the Advisory Council (Shura) proposes its recommendations to the President and concerned ministries and submits them to the People's Assembly. The judicial authority has complete autonomy. The press has also become autonomous according to the Constitution since it both expresses public opinion and creates it. The Higher Press Council enjoys a considerable position as an autonomous institution for press affairs.

The Arab Republic of Egypt is divided into administrative units, viz. the governorates, and towns and villages which conform to the principle of local rule. Each governorate has an executive council headed by a governor, and an elected People's Assembly. The towns and villages each have a People's Assembly whose members are elected, in addition to the executive councils which represent the executive power. All the governors and chairmen of the local People's Assembly in the governorates participate in a Higher Council for local rule headed by the Prime Minister.

Egypt enjoys diplomatic relations with most countries of the world and affirms its adherence to the Arab, Islamic and African world. It is a member state in the United Nations, international organizations, a member of the Afro-Asian Conference, the organization for African Unity and the Non-Aligned States.

2.4   Social Structure

Egyptian society is divided into rural and urban communities. The rural community represents the largest segment of the society and was the fundamental social structure for thousands of years, during which Egyptians had to face annual floods and exploited this water for agriculture. Farming is the vocation of nearly half of the Egyptian labour force, accounting for 4,878,623 farmers or 47.7% of the workforce in 1976.

The rural communities have a specific character imposed by the nature of agriculture and farming, which involves positive and negative aspects. The positive aspects are reflected in the family structure and bond, which extends over two generations, in which the authority of the elders is respected by the younger family members. Villagers live in a community setting in which the younger members serve and attend to elders in addition to taking counsel from them. Negative aspects of village life are apathy and disdain for the value of time.

Rural areas in Egypt suffer from certain problems and economically cultivation is restrained and per capita income is inadequate. According to statistics, per capita income was 82.3 Egyptian pounds in 1975, and owners of less than five feddans numbered 3,033,000 individuals or 94.5% of the population in 1972. Underemployment and seasonal unemployment is another problem which affects almost 10.5 million individuals aged sixteen and over in a population of 20 million, or 54.6%. Unemployment falls to 40% when the working age is defined as beginning at age fifteen. The unemployment problem has resulted in one bread-winner supporting three additional individuals at a rate of 2.97%.

In spite of the efforts made since 1952 to improve social and health conditions in rural areas and to install electricity and running water, rural areas remain much less developed than urban areas. The rate of illiteracy is still high and in spite of bringing certain epidemic diseases under control, local diseases such as bilharzia and anclistoma still exist. Structures are also lacking for cultural and leisure activities.

The urban areas of Egypt are the cities which have existed since antiquity such as Memphis, Thebes (presently Luxor) and Alexandria, along with cities which sprang up in the Middle Ages such as Cairo (presently the capital and the largest city in Africa) and modern cities which were created with the inauguration of the Suez Canal in 1896, namely Port Said, Ismailia and Suez. There are also cities which have become the capitals of governorates, as well as the small towns, which are widespread centres of civilization in the rural areas. Other towns which grew up during and after the industrial movement in Egypt in the mid-nineteenth century have witnessed such industries as textiles and weaving, and oil and oil refining in the towns of Mehalla Al Kubia and Kafr-el Zayat. About 4.8 million individuals in the total working population are concentrated in Egyptian cities, representing 43.3% according to 1976 statistics.

The urban areas are generally characterised by a higher per capita income than the rural areas, representing an average of 170.5 Egyptian pounds in 1975, and by the role of attraction they constitute for the population as a result of the advantages they offer. Industrial and economic activity is concentrated in the urban areas, as are administrations, government agencies and educational institutions of various levels, especially with regard to the university and higher education. The cities also offer cultural, artistic and entertainment activities.

In spite of the endeavours of the government to decentralize local rule, internal emigration from rural to urban areas is a current phenomenon, especially in Cairo and Alexandria, which are the two major poles of civilization as well as centres for industry, trade and services. Further, Cairo is an industrial city and the nation's capital and Alexandria is the second major city and a seaport. The effects of emigration are demonstrated by the following data:

- A rapid increase in the population, in Cairo and Alexandria in particular and in other cities in general. The population of Cairo increased from 1,312,000 in 1937 to 2,091,000 in 1947, from 2,724,290 in 1957 to 3,298,882 in 1960, and from 5,074,017 in 1976 to 5,803,000 in 1982. With the population of Giza and some of the suburbs which presently form Greater Cairo, the population is approximately ten million inhabitants. As for Alexandria, the population increased over the same periods from 686,000 to 919,000, from 1,227,829 to 1,497,026 and from 2,317,705 to 2,664,000.

- Population density in Cairo is such that 27 thousand inhabitants were living in one square kilometre in 1982. In Alexandria the density was 13 thousand per one square kilometre according to 1947 statistics. This average has decreased by half since 1960 as a result of the addition of new areas to those cities, bringing the figure to approximately 994 inhabitants per square kilometre in 1982.

- Population density is high in the old quarters of both cities since they are the areas most densely inhabited by the emigrants from rural areas. Emigrants have also settled in surrounding areas of the city, in which they have reconstituted their original environment with the same rural customs and traditions.

Among the major problems facing internal emigration is the incapacity of those cities to offer real employment opportunities. The unemployed population in the cities totals approximately 8.7 million or 45.4% of the total unemployed Egyp-

tian population. Underemployment in the Administration is one
of the major aspects of unemployment in Egyptian cities. Another aspect is a lack of public services.

Egypt is faced with a major social problem, namely the
increase in the population, which is due to a number of factors
among which are the following:

- A high birth rate since the beginning of this century;
  between 1930 and the early seventies ranging from 39%
  to approximately 34.3%.

- A gradual decrease in the mortality rate, especially
  among newborns, as a result of improved health
  and social care. The mortality rate decreased from
  25.7% to 14.9% during the above-mentioned period.

- As a result of the two above-mentioned factors, a
  natural increase in the population ocurred from 1.8%
  in the thirties to approximately 2.54% in the early
  seventies.

- Both the birth rate and early marriages have increased,
  in particular in the rural areas.

- The increase of the average individual's age.

The following table indicates trends in the growth of
the Egyptian population:

Table 1

Population Growth in Egypt

Year	Population	Annual Increase in %
1927	14 177 864	1.09
1937	15 950 694	1.16
1947	18 966 764	1.81
1960	26 080 000	2.39
1976	36 626 204	2.53
1982 (estimate)	45 000 000	3.80

The table indicates the following:

- Egypt has witnessed steady population growth since the early sixties and culminating in the seventies, reaching 8,373,796 in the six years from 1976 to 1982.

- Population growth in Egypt reached 3.8% in 1982 whereas such a rate never exceeds 1% in developed countries.

- When adding the sparsely populated areas, we notice that the density rate increased to 818 inhabitants per square kilometre. Egypt is facing economic problems which require a scientific solution on the part of the State, such as the redistribution of the population, creation of new communities and land reform.

- The expansion of the urban area of greater Cairo by the addition of the Giza sector, the town of Shubra El Kheima and the villages of Giza governorate results in a population of almost ten million inhabitants.

2.5   Education

The Egyptian Constitution stipulates that education is free of charge since it is every citizen's right to obtain it. Education has witnessed different types of development. In the fifties, education was legally divided into the following stages:

- *The primary stage,* for a period of six years.

- *The intermediate stage,* for a period of three years.

- *The secondary stage,* for a period of three years, divided into academic education, industrial education, commercial education, agricultural education and teacher training.

- *Higher and university education.*

- *Post-graduate education.*

Religious education at the Azhar still follows this scale.

According to Law No. 139 of 1981, education was transformed as follows:

- *Basic education*, for a period of nine years, from 6 to 15 years of age. It is a compulsory stage preceded by an optional two years of kindergarten.

- *The secondary stage*, for a period of three years, from 15 to 18 years of age. This stage is divided into the academic general secondary stage and the technical secondary stage, which includes an industrial section and a commercial section, in addition to an agricultural section. It also includes a school for the training of male and female teachers for the primary stage.

- *Higher and university education*, according to the university law, is pursued by those who have received the general secondary certificate and by outstanding graduates from the technical secondary stage. Universities grant degrees and diplomas to graduates, and postgraduate degrees such as masters degrees and doctorates.

This education law came as a result of studies concerning the education situation and the prerequisites of development and modernization. The fundamental principles for the modernization of education are as follows:

- Education for the establishment of democracy.

- Education for comprehensive development and productive work.

- Education within the framework of Arab cultural autonomy.

- Education within the framework of lifelong education.

The Ministry of Education drew up a working plan for the achievement of the principles as follows:

- "Widen the scope of education and increase its institutions to avoid limiting it to formal education in its traditional form and extend it for the benefit of religious, social, economic, co-operative, productive, trade union, community, informative and political institutions so as to contribute to the training and education orientation of the society.

- Remove the barriers between formal and nonformal education in the light of a comprehensive outlook for the purpose of preparing individuals and providing them with a number and a variety of education opportunities.

- Develop the potentials of self-education as an important objective of lifelong education. This is feasible by providing the basics of education through formal education, thus enabling individuals to continue their education in different fields and specializations according to their particular capacities.

- Provide economic and social incentives to promote the continuation of education."

Beginning with the academic year 1980-81, the Ministry of Education adopted a comprehensive strategy for the development of education in quality and in quantity, with the aim of making it available to everyone. The Ministry's concern is to provide adults with education opportunities, especially for illiterates, and special concentration in deprived sectors and new communities. The aim is also to provide individuals with continuous education opportunities in the form of formal and nonformal institutions.

A number of executive programmes and plans were drawn up for this strategy among which are the following:

Development of Basic Education

This aims at extending the period of compulsory education encompassing the primary and intermediate stages for a period of nine years. This stage became an integral part with the aim of providing learners with the necessary ethics, behaviour, knowledge and practical skills adapted to different kinds of environments and allowing those who have ended their basic education to embark on life or continue their education at higher stages.

Illiteracy and relapse into it may be controlled once this form of education is comprehensive among children aged 6 to 15, so opportunities to continue education whether in formal or nonformal schools will be possible.

The specific objectives defined by the Ministry of Education are as follows: "Gradually increase enrolment until it is complete within an adequate system of education according to the principle of equal opportunities for all which is a pillar of democracy and the right of every citizen."

Reinforcement of Nonformal Education

Lifelong education is a priority of the present social, economic, scientific and technological development of Egypt and the world at large. It requires the integration of nonformal education institutions with formal institutions so as to provide education opportunities equivalent to school education for whoever did not receive it previously, such as drop-outs and neo-literates who would like to join a formal institute or benefit from nonformal education programmes.

The Ministry of Education submitted a working paper for the development and modernization of education in Egypt stipulating the following:

Nonformal education encompasses all the endeavours for the education of those who received very little education and care to increase their knowledge when working. It also encompasses those who consider the continuation of education as necessary in order to keep up with the current changes in vocational structures. Efforts are thus exerted in developing local communities, vocational training, agricultural guidance, labour culture, public culture, child education, women's education, health education, demographic and environmental education and finally adult training programmes whether before or during work. Directive programmes include the realization of investing spare time in a better manner and in making use of environmental potentials.

Literacy programmes are a priority for this form of education since illiteracy is a major problem in Egypt as a result of foreign occupation and social repression prior to 1952.

In our opinion, illiteracy is not limited to the inability to read and write; cultural, vocational and political illiteracy also exist.

The Ministry of Education set out a group of programmes for that purpose which include the following:

- Gradually raise the enrolment rate in basic education as a way of impeding the causes of illiteracy and raise the standard of this form of education, restrict the phenomenon of drop-outs so as to prevent a relapse into illiteracy and establish a one-class school for those who did not have the opportunity to enrol in a basic education school. Therefore, basic formal and adult education are integrated.

- Draw up a national literacy plan.

- Design functional programmes for women's education.

2.6   Education Administration

According to the local rule implemented in Egypt, the education administration combines both the principles of centralization and decentralization as the central organizations review the policies, planning, co-ordination, follow-up and evaluation when the complete responsibility of the implementation has been assigned to local organizations, which in turn also collaborate on decision making at a national level throughout periodical meetings with the chairmen of the education administrations and the responsible education institutions in the governorates. This is undertaken in order to study the general problems faced by local administrations and find adequate solutions in the form of a combined education policy and a public opinion consensus.

Within the framework of the centralization of planning and the decentralization of implementation, the Ministry charged the education directorates in the governorates with the following responsibilities:

- Define the timetable of courses and holidays adapted to local circumstances, provided the academic year of no less than eight months is respected.

- Supervise transition exams at all stages, the different types of education, final exams at the fundamental basic education stage and follow-up general certificate exams such as the general secondary exam and technical school diplomas.

- Define the enrolment rate in teaching institutes and

employ graduates.

- Provide authorizations for the construction of schools (except for the general secondary stage and its equivalents) according to the general education plan and the requisites of governorates.

The necessary procedures to provide teachers, guides and administrative employees at the governorate level are also undertaken.

2.7   Quantitative Development at the Different Education Levels

Fundamental Education Statistics

- The enrolment rate of children aged 12 to 16 years accounted for 46% of school-age children prior to the revolution of 1952; it increased in 1984 to 92.7%. The number of children enroled in the first form of basic education, including the primary Azhar Institute, totalled 1,117,118 pupils in a total of 1,205,000 children aged 6 to 7. Thus Egyptian society is moving rapidly towards full enrolment.

- 639,088 pupils have been accepted in the seventh form of basic education from 664,005 who have succeeded in passing through the sixth form, a rate of 99.2%. However, attention is to be given to avoid failures and drop-outs and to prevent a relapse into illiteracy.

- The number of children who studied in the first cycle of basic education (the first six years) totalled 5,680,528 in the academic year 1984-85 from a total of 7,041,185 children, or 80.68%. If the pupils of the Azhar primary institutes were added the rate would be 85%.

- The number of pupils in the second cycle of basic education (seventh, eighth and ninth form) totalled 2,000,087 in the academic year 1984-85 from a total of 3,428,416 children aged 12 to 15, or 85.35%.

- The number of pupils at the basic education stage totalled 7,680,615 in the academic year 1984-85 from a total of 10,469,601 children aged 6 to 15, 73.35%.

The figures indicate that 35% of pupils are exposed to relapsing into illiteracy after having ended the first stage of basic education. Those pupils can be saved if they are provided with nonformal education programmes to assist them in retaining the skills they acquired as well as in having the opportunities to continue their education. This group, however, should have priority in the post-literacy programmes along with neo-literates, even though the programmes will differ in content and syllabus in view of the age difference.

Secondary Education

The present education policy aims at expanding technical education on the one hand and general secondary education on the other in order to prepare leavers to face their practical and vocational life and to prepare them to enrol in higher and university institutions.

In 1978-79, the Ministry of Education began to experiment and promote the system of a comprehensive school, which would integrate academic education with technical and vocational education. The syllabus would include a group of compulsory subjects and another optional group of subjects permitting flexibility, and one or two vocational courses for the pupil to follow during the stage of basic education.

Secondary and technical education are combined in order to prepare skilled workers and technicians.

Five-year technical schools have been experimented with by the Ministry of Education with the aim of qualifying technicians and supervisors in commercial, industrial and agricultural fields. Ninety new specializations were introduced by the Ministry in technical education, in addition to a number of specialized courses. The five-year technical schools were expanded in order to qualify technicians in 38 other specializations.

The number of students enrolled in secondary education schools of different types, in addition to institutes for male and female teachers, during the academic year 1984-85 is indicated in the following table:

Table 2

Number of Students Enrolled in the Different

Types of Secondary Education

Type of Education	Number of Students Enrolled
General Secondary	563 792
Technical Industrial Secondary	251 458
Technical Agricultural Secondary	95 689
Technical Commercial Secondary	455 700
Institute for Male and Female Teachers	77 535

The number of students accepted in the first form of the secondary diversified stage totalled 472.896 in the academic year 1984-1985 from a total of 511,493 students holding certificates of the intermediate stage. The enrolment rate is therefore 92.5%.

Public Religious Education at the Azhar

The number of students and institutes in the primary, intermediate and secondary stages of education and the public religious institutes at the Azhar during the academic year 1982-83 is indicated in the following table:

Table 3

Number of Students Enrolled in Public

Religious Institutes at the Azhar

Stage	Number of Institutes	Number of Students
Primary	600	144 927
Intermediate for boys	311	54 352
Intermediate for girls	89	15 250
Secondary for boys	179	15 182
Secondary for girls	71	19 864
Institute for teachers	18	6 327
Institute for reading	19	2 468

University and Higher Education

Until 1951-52, Egypt had only three universities, namely Cairo University (1908), Alexandria University (1942) and Ein Shams University (1950), whereas there are presently eleven universities, which include approximately 113 higher institutes.

The number of students enrolled in universities (excluding the Azhar University) rose from 35,056 students in 1951-52 to 558,527 students in 1980-81; the Azhar University had 65,451 students during the same period.

There are technical institutes in higher education which are affiliated with the Ministry of Higher Education and are responsible for qualifying technicians in the fields of commerce and industry. There are 17 higher institutes of commerce with an enrolment of 64,870 students in 1982 registered for twelve specializations, and 16 technical institutes of industry with an enrolment of 22,341 students in 1982. There are also private higher institutes which differ according to period of studies and specialization, as well as one private university, the American University in Cairo.

3.   THE DEVELOPMENT STAGES OF LITERACY IN EGYPT

3.1   First Stage: 1919-1952

Certain pioneers in education at the time of the Egyptian renaissance in the early nineteenth century, during the
reign of Mohamed Aly, pointed out the problem of illiteracy and
put forward the modern system of education in Egypt at that
time by making education compulsory during the first stage and
demanding that it be free of charge. However, this was not implemented at that time, although volunteer efforts by benevo-
lent associations and political parties did establish schools
and classes for literacy education. Nevertheless, all these
efforts died off with the British occupation at the end of the
last century and this situation continued until the Constitution of 1923. The Compulsory Education Law was issued in 1924
and began to be implemented in 1925. This law had a strong
impact in promoting education and gave impetus to the literacy
movement which led to the opening of certain schools by political parties in 1907. Meanwhile the Ministry of Education opened
night schools in 1923 for the literacy education of different
groups and the development of skills. It opened three types of
schools: night schools managed by the Ministry of Education,
other schools managed by the Council of Governorates and a
third type of school managed by the citizens themselves.

Learners in those schools were assigned to classes according to different vocations and skills: farmers, small industry owners and others. Their ages ranged from under fifteen
to over thirty-five.

The literacy campaign witnessed a period of development

and flourished from 1922 to the second half of the twentieth
century as a result of the nationalist movement which occurred
after the revolution of 1919 and the establishment of the Constitution and the Compulsory Education Law. The law aimed at
promoting education by creating compulsory schools and public
libraries for the six years of education from age 7 to 13. However, these schools offered no education level since they were
basically aimed at the poorer population and those working in
sectors such as farming and industry. The aim was to promote the
continuity of those skills among the young. Therefore, education in these schools was limited to half days or uses the two
period system, i.e. one group of children goes in the morning
and another attends in the afternoon, whereas another form of
primary education relied on an entrance exam and payment of
fees, with pupils in that form of education moving on to other
education stages.

Compulsory schools opened their doors three times daily,
in the morning and in the afternoon for children, and in the
evening for adults. Many teachers volunteered to instruct
adults, and both the Ministry of Education and the Council of
Governorates financed more classes in order to bring them to
every province. The education programmes implemented in those
schools included the basics of reading, writing, arithmetic,
religion, health and ethics.

Egypt was affected by the economic crisis of the thirties,
which devastated the world, and the enthusiasm for education
died off until 1944 when Law No. 110 was issued. A new era began with this law which was the first literacy education legislation issued in Egypt, the Arab world and Africa. The law was
the crowning of all the previous efforts and came as a result
of new social awareness following World War II, necessitating
measures to put an end to ignorance, poverty and illness. The
newly created Ministry of Social Affairs was given the responsibility of implementing the literacy law and spreading popular
culture.

The articles stipulated in the law organised the major
aspects of literacy work, first by defining an illiterate and
establishing all the rules, such as the syllabus, duration,
schedule, teachers and their qualification, specifications, and
the evaluation of learners. The administrative units and supervisory bodies were also defined.

By Law No. 128 in 1946 the responsibility for literacy

work was transferred from the Ministry of Social Affairs to the Ministry of Education, which immediately created a special central department for literacy to supervise the literacy units and co-ordinate the work between the Ministry and the different committees. An important modification was introduced into the law concerning the age of illiterates which made it possible for school-age children who could not find a vacancy in an education establishment to attend literacy classes.

After Law No. 110 was issued in 1944, the Ministry of Social Affairs scientifically oriented certain experimental projects on a small scale in rural and urban areas in order to cope with the prerequisites of literacy in its practical reality. The city of Cairo and certain departments of the Giza governorate were selected for the implementation of these projects. During the academic year 1945-46, a literacy campaign began for policemen in Cairo, and classes were opened in the Giza governorate. However, this project had no effect on the syllabus, programme or organization of work, or on academic plans.

When responsibility for implementation was transfered to the Ministry of Education, it was actually carried out and no longer remained confined to an experimental framework. Organizational departments were created in the country to assist other institutions in creating special literacy units.

Because of the dimension of illiteracy (5 million illiterates at that time) and the small budget, the Ministry of Education drew up its priorities concerning age, sex and the period of education. The period of education was decreased from two years to one. According to statistics, in spite of the considerable efforts made, only 4.5% of illiterates obtained literacy skills over a period of ten years.

The popular university was created for the first time in Egypt in 1945 for post-literacy education. The university's objective is the adult education of individuals of both sexes who want to increase their knowledge, vocational orientation or general culture. Branches of this university have been established in the regional capitals of Egypt, with itinerant cultural units operating in the villages. The popular university was largely acclaimed at the time it began.

In 1946, 3,300 students were enrolled. It was also known as the popular cultural institution in 1949 and was entirely re-organised, incorporating commercial schools, and was wide-

spread in Cairo and in the governorates. The university included twenty departments and many specializations, with 15,660
enrolled learners in 1951-52.

3.2   Second Stage: 1953-1969

At the time the second stage began, no legislation had
been issued for literacy since Law No. 110 of 1944, which was
still applied with its revisions and executive regulations.
However, certain laws were issued concerning the management of
primary education after the 1952 revolution; these had a considerable impact on decreasing the rate of illiteracy. Law No.
210 issued in 1952 stipulated that primary education is compulsory and free of charge for all children aged 6 to 12; nevertheless, certain modifications were introduced in the law in
1956 and 1968.

Executive endeavours went on during this period at two
levels: at the government level and at the joint level between
the government and international organizations.

One of the main modifications introduced in the law
during the sixties was the concept of a comprehensive national
plan. As a result of population growth, an increase of
12,587,686 illiterates occurred at a rate of 69.7% according to
1960 statistics; this is more than half the population. The
State, therefore, drew up a comprehensive plan to end illiteracy between 1962 and 1975. The plan, however, was not implemented, and an alternative plan was proposed to end illiteracy
between 1965 and 1979, that is, a fifteen-year plan instead of
a thirteen-year plan; it also met with failure.

Separate projects, however, were implemented, including
popular schools for the literacy education of 820,000 illiterates residing in Cairo. Scheduled for a period of eight to nine
years, it lasted only five years and assured the literacy of
approximately 195,000 learners. The same experimental project
was implemented in Alexandria for the literacy of workers in
economic and industrial sectors. The project lasted from 1964
to 1966.

*Joint Endeavours by the Egyptian Government and
International Organizations (ASFEC)*

Numerous projects have been carried out jointly by the

Egyptian government and regional and international organizations. Unesco is the major organization, through the Secretariat in Paris and its Regional Centre for Adult Education, ASFEC, which has the following role:

The Regional Centre for Adult Education (formerly the Arab States Fundamental Education Centre), ASFEC, was established in Sirs Al Layan in the governorate of Menufia in 1952 following the agreement signed between the Egyptian Government and Unesco. The Centre aims to train teachers of fundamental education, to provide the necessary education material and to undertake adequate technical research for the development of fundamental education in Arab States. The centre pursued work in this field until 1959, however its functions changed to community development and it continued to provide training, conduct research and furnish educational material and technical counsel at the time the Centre was expanded to include functional literacy in 1969, and later adult education beginning in 1982. This broadened the horizons of nonformal education.

Before noting the functions of the Centre (ASFEC) in developing education strategies, it is worthwhile to point out the vital and pioneering role of the Centre in preparing general strategies aimed at coping with the problem of illiteracy in the Arab states. Two strategies have been put forward to be worked upon by the Centre and it is important to separate them.

The first set of strategies is concerned with general policy and planning, known in the field of literacy as "the art of organizing relations linking literacy policies to planning and practices in order to coincide the effort deployed with political purposes". The Centre has proposed a strategy for literacy in the Arab world according to studies and reports concerning seventeen Arab states.

The second set of strategies is concerned with methods of education. The Centre put forth many efforts in the literacy and post-literacy stages, while employing many different strategies for the purpose of preparing and testing subjects for model education or self-education strategies, or village libraries, as follows:

The Centre developed a large variety of educational materials for the literacy and post-literacy stages. This was a pioneering achievement for the Arab world and in particular for Egypt, which, since the Centre was established in Egypt, had the privilege of having its environment selected for adapted study. In the fifties, a series of basic books were published by the Centre to teach reading and writing of which the series I Read, and I Count, as well as *The Teacher's Manual* were specific to literacy. Another series for follow-up of the post-literacy stage was published, including *Our Arab Nation, Our Daily Life, Our Feasts and Celebrations, Our Heroes, Your Health, Humor and Advice, Our New Society, The Successful Farmer and Customs and Traditions*. The books were all adapted to learners who had completed literacy classes to help them continue to read and prevent relapse into illiteracy.

The *Sakia* newspaper was circulated by the Centre and represented an example of the learning strategies for the post-literacy stage. This panel newspaper was intended for the newly emancipated farmers who would participate in editing and printing the newspaper using a simplified method adapted to their education level.

According to experiments and research conducted by the Centre in vocational training, a number of suitable books were prepared in the late seventies for the post-literacy stage. These will be discussed in more detail following discussion of the training centres for construction.

In 1982, the Centre organized a meeting at the first specialized seminar under the title "The Preparation and Production of Educational Materials for Neo-literates". At the seminar, which was attended by twenty-four representatives from Arab and African states, six booklets for the post-literacy stage were prepared and tested. Two booklets were in Arabic, two in English and two others in French. They were intended for neo-literate learners in rural areas in the different fields of development adapted to Arab and African states.

The Centre has taken a special interest in rural libraries as a learning strategy. A model library was created in Sirs Al Layan and used for training. It offers technical assistance for primary and secondary school libraries and community centre libraries in neighbouring villages.

A field study was undertaken by the Centre in 1978 to find the best form of library services adaptable to the region and to become acquainted with the reading habits of its inhabitants in order to provide libraries with suitable books. In other words, the study aimed at answering two central questions:

first, is a permanent library better than a mobile one? Second, what are the subjects, topics and levels that should be available in those libraries?

Two villages were studied in the Menufia Municipality, in which a permanent library was created in one village and a mobile library in a specially equipped car for the other village. Both libraries were provided with the same books on various subjects, adapted and balanced for the rural community. The study and results were published by the Centre in Arabic.

The Centre also conducted another experiment in the seventies for strategies of self-learning for illiterates during the basic stage which is also useful in many aspects for post-literacy education and continuing education. The Centre produced for that purpose a series of nine booklets entitled *Teach Yourself*, with four cassette tapes to assist illiterates in acquiring the reading, writing and arithmetic skills up to the fourth grade of the primary stage.

Throughout the thirty years of its existance, ASFEC has played a considerable role at the international, national and regional levels in preparing training guides for literacy education in the Arab states and in contributing to intensifying and propagating the functional concept in Egypt through its studies and research. Thanks to those efforts, the concept was not limited to vocational training but extended to meet the social, economic and individual requirements of adults, and assure reading, writing and arithmetic skills.

The Centre continues to function at the national and Arab levels, and recently its activity has extended to African and Asian countries. In 1982 the Centre was transferred to the Egyptian administration.

3.3   Third Stage: 1970-1985

In 1970 Law No. 67 was issued for literacy and adult education concerning the management, planning and financing of this form of education on a new basis as follows:

- Literacy and adult education is a political and national obligation.

- The aim of literacy and adult education is to educate

and raise the cultural and vocational levels of citizens.

- All government bodies and political organizations are committed to the implementation of the law in coopera- tion with the Ministry of Education.

In accordance with this law, Republican Decree No. 311 was issued in 1971 with a view to the formation of the Higher Committee for Literacy and Adult Education: for the purpose of defining its functions in planning literacy work, the priori- ties and requisites of implementation, and the human and finan- cial capacities and incentives, for the purpose of indicating the methods of financing it as well as the co-ordination ar- rangements between different specific work sectors and, finally, for the purpose of following up the implementation of the work- ing plan in its different stages.

The modification of the Constitution, which adopted the principle of many parties and local rule, confirms the role of local organizations for implementation and central organiza- tions for planning, follow-up and reinforcement. Therefore Law No. 67 of 1970 was revised and replaced by Law No. 40 of 1982. The new law assigned the implementation of literacy to local rule units, public organizations, political and popular insti- tutions, companies and so forth, working through the Council of Ministers. A Council of Governorates under the chairmanship of the governor for the executive aspect of literacy was also affirmed by the law. The Higher Council for Adult and Literacy Education underwent reform according to Decree No. 947 of the Council of Ministers in 1982, which includes the participation of experts in that field as well as representatives of all political parties in Egypt. Finally, Republican Decree No. 19 was issued in 1985 to organize the National Population Council to be headed by the President of the Republic, who is respon- sible for keeping the illiteracy rate under control.

Beyond the legislative aspect, two projects concerning implementation were drawn up after the issuance of Law No. 67 in 1970. The first project aimed at rapidly eradicating il- literacy among government and public sector workers, who ac- counted for 195,000 illiterates during the period 1972-73 and 1975-76. The second project was aimed at literacy in the pri- vate sector, which accounted for approximately 10 million il- literates between the ages of 10 and 45 in 1973. Implementation of the projects was estimated for a period of seven years, 1973-1974 and 1979-1980.

Implementation of the first project was assigned to ministries, institutions, establishments, organizations and companies in the public sector which finance it. The second project was undertaken by the Ministry of Education. However, the results of both projects were quite poor.

4. THE PRESENT SITUATION OF LITERACY AND POST-LITERACY
   EDUCATION ENDEAVOURS

4.1 The Extent of Illiteracy Problems

The following table indicates the rate of illiteracy in
Egypt according to various census years:

Table 4

Number and Proportion of Illiterates in Egypt

According to Census Year

Year of Census	Male illiterates Number	Rate	Female illiterates Number	Rate	Total	Total Rate
1937	4 468 422	76.6%	5 416 858	93.9%	9 885 280	85.2%
1947	4 443 384	64.3%	5 964 624	84.3%	10 407 972	74.5%
1960	5 048 662	56.2%	7 539 024	83.1%	12 587 686	69.7%
1966	5 591 000	50.0%	8 072 000	76.0%	13 373 000	63.0%
1976	5 726 187	42.0%	9 368 828	71.0%	15 094 015	56.0%

The table indicates the following:

- The illiteracy rate has generally decreased slowly,
  therefore the extent of the problem has in fact increased with population growth.

- According to statistics, female illiteracy is higher
  than male illiteracy.

- The decrease in the illiteracy rate is slower among females than among males.

The latest statistics, from 1976, indicate that the rate of illiteracy is generally higher with advanced age groups, as a result of widespread education among the younger age groups, and has to do with a past lack of interest in education, which has led to illiteracy as indicated in the following table:

Table 5

Rate of Illiteracy by Age Group in 1976

Age group	Rate of illiteracy		Total
	Male	Female	
under 10	26%	48%	36%
11-15	36%	57%	46%
16-20	42%	73%	58%
21-40	52%	87%	69%
60 and older	65%	92%	79%
TOTAL	42%	71%	56%

The table also shows that the rate of illiteracy is still high among the productive age group (21-40 years), viz. 69%.

The statistics also indicate an increase in the illiteracy rates in rural areas as compared to urban areas, at a rate of 70.6% and 39.7% respectively.

The findings of the estimate made at a later date indicate a noticeable decrease in the illiteracy rate as indicated in the following table:

Table 6

Estimation of the Illiteracy Rate in Egypt

from 1977 to 1981

Year of Estimation	Male and Female		Rural and Urban		Total
	Male	Female	Rural	Urban	
1977	41.1%	70.4%	69.8%	38.6%	55.5%
1978	40.3%	69.9%	69.2%	38.2%	54.9%
1979	39.6%	69.4%	68.6%	37.7%	54.2%
1980	38.8%	68.9%	68.0%	37.3%	53.6%
1981	38.0%	68.5%	67.4%	36.9%	52.9%

National Literacy Plan

According to the findings, the Higher Council for Adult and Literacy Education, under its new structure, formed a technical committee which prepared the project for the National Literacy Plan while taking into consideration the co-ordination of endeavours between different locations and proposing the establishment of new complementary location. The role of each establishment has been defined so as to effect the integration and take advantage of the potentials of each organization and institution.

The plan aims at ending illiteracy or at least limiting it within a short period so as to raise the capacity and productivity of the illiterate once he reaches working age, as well as to apply the principle of equal education opportunities for all. Illiteracy is tackled comprehensively, as far as reading and writing are concerned, and with a view to cultural and vocational literacy. Different organizations, political parties, trade unions, popular institutions and educated individuals must contribute to ending illiteracy, which is a national problem.

The proposed plan is divided into two parts:

Part One:

It aims at eliminating sources of illiteracy by striving to increase enrolment rates and resolve the problem of regression and drop-outs. This must also be accompanied by necessary measures of gradual education for those who did not have the opportunity to receive an education, as well as for drop-outs

and school-age children, by means of the endeavours put forth
by certain institutions and organizations of nonformal education, such as one-class schools or vocational training centres.
This part of the plan aims at those in the 6-15 age group who
never enrolled in school and at drop-outs. There were approximately 2,279,000 children in that situation in 1982-1983.

Part Two:

It aims at the literacy education of those who are fifteen years of age and older, who are above the normal school
attendance age and who have not acquired a basic education
certificate and are either totally or partially illiterate.
Two age groups have been defined in the plan and are alter-
nately selected during the implementation of the plan. The
first group is the 15-35 age group; approximately 9,254,000 or
52.9% are illiterate according to 1983-84 literacy estimates.
Of the figure, 3,344,750 are male illiterates (38%) and
5,909,500 (68.5%) are female illiterates. The second group is
the 15-45 age group. According to 1983-84 population estimates,
there are 11,518, 890 illiterates, of which 4,163,090 are males
and 7,355,800 are females, reflecting the same proportions as
above.

The quantitative aims of the plan, in view of what has
been discussed, is to achieve the literacy education of the
above-mentioned groups in ten to twelve years' time, with
priority given to the following groups:

- Male youths who are nearing military service age
  (15-20 years of age).

- Illiterate workers in the government and the public
  sector.

- Illiterates in the private sector in the 15-35 or
  15-45 age groups.

- Women and the rural population.

As for the qualitative aim of the plan, it is the at-
tainment of a functional level by learners. This is the level
at which the learner employs his reading, writing and arithmetic skills in order to continue further education, for self-
expression and to be able to use education in practical life.
Thus learners may acquire the capacity to take part in cultural
activities, contribute actively to creating a civilization and

to interact with society. This plan differs from other plans in that this level is the equivalent of the sixth primary grade rather than the fourth primary grade, which was the level in other plans.

According to this plan, education was divided into three levels:

First Level:

Full illiterates join the first level and complete the curriculum, which is 900 hours over 18 months.

Second Level:

This level is for those who know the alphabet and possess the basics of reading, writing and arithmetic. The curriculum is covered in 600 hours over 12 months.

Third Level:

This level is specific to those who read and write with difficulty. Included in this level are large numbers of persons who have relapsed into illiteracy or who received a literacy certificate but whose skills are weak, and housewives who attended primary schools in the past. The curriculum is covered in 300 hours over six months.

However, the plan is still under research, and alternatives are currently being studied.

4.2   The Present Curriculum

Currently, the curriculum aims at promoting learners to the level equivalent to the fourth primary grade by having them attend literacy classes for a full academic year (nine months). As a result of the incessant need for and concentration on the education of certain groups of society as well as for development, four academic books were published for the literacy classes.

The books, which have taken into consideration the different requirements of learners according to the various environments, are as follows:

- Basic reading book for the agricultural environment

This book teaches reading and writing to illiterates living in rural areas. The topics vary and deal with the agricultural environment, in addition to cultural, national, social, health and environmental topics.

- Basic reading book for the industrial environment

It includes vocational and industrial topics in addition to certain cultural and ethical aspects.

- Arithmetic book for adult education

This book is used for both agricultural and industrial environments.

- General culture book

This book includes different units which are taught by teachers in co-operation with certain experts. Religious, national, social, health and general knowledge topics are included.

With the modification of literacy aims, the books, educational materials and curriculum are presently being revised. The Higher Council for Literacy and Adult Education has agreed on methods for use in preparing learners to reach the level of the sixth primary grade instead of the fourth grade while observing the functional aspect in preparing the curriculum, selecting the context and preparing the educational materials.

4.3   Learning Strategies in the Post-literacy Stage and Lifelong Education

The General Theoretical Framework

In 1980, the Ministry of Education, as previously mentioned, issued a document for the development and modernization of education in Egypt. The current social, economic, scientific and technological development of our society requires that education be continuing. Therefore, this implies the integration of a nonformal system of education with a formal system in order to offer all the educational opportunities to attain the same level or complete school education.

Nonformal education is viewed by this document as an endeavour to assist learners who have received a limited amount of education and who wish to increase it once they enter a vocation and those who find it necessary to continue their education in order to keep pace with rapid changes in vocational structures.

According to the Islamic concept of lifelong education, which has been discussed previously in this document, and since Islam is the official religion in Egypt, many studies, experiments and endeavours have been undertaken in Egypt to encompass all the learning strategies in post-literacy and continuing education.

Before discussing the strategies, it is necessary to point out that learning strategy means learning techniques and methods and not what is generally understood by strategy in political and military terms.

Learning strategies are still employed in Egypt, in other words numerous learning methods are used, including:

Newspapers and Magazines

ASFEC, the Regional Centre for Adult Education, was the first to issue a magazine entitled *Al Sakia,* specially designed for an agricultural environment. This example was followed by other Arab states which issued similar magazines.

A weekly magazine named *Co-operation,* for farmers and workers, was later issued with separate literacy education pages for neo-literates, with large print-type and a simplified language covering information of special interest to this group.

The daily Egyptian press and magazines have simplified the language in allotted sections so as to allow neo-literates to read the news. The space made available is divided into subjects concerning various groups such as women, youth, workers and farmers, and space has been allotted to news concerning municipalities. This method has succeeded in widening readership.

Textual Materials Prepared for Post-literacy Studies

Egypt was the first country in the world to invent writing and create public libraries. Books were made of rolls of papyrus, and the Alexandria library, which is the most ancient library in history preserved the ancient Greek culture and civilization, as well as translations of many other civilizations. Christian monasteries have also played a pioneering role in preserving papyrus documents of Egyptian civilization.

Islam honoured books and more than three hundred times the word "book" was mentioned in the Koran. The Muslims named the Koran "The Book" because it was the first book written in Arabic; its writing began in the mid-Hegire century, reaching a zenith in the third and fourth Hegire centuries. This led Ibn Nadim to collect all the Arab works in what is known as the first Arabic bibliography in history. Libraries spread to mosques, palaces, houses and stationary shops commonly visited by most authors of the time.

Printing was introduced in Egypt with the French campaign in 1798. Small printing presses flourished and continued to operate until 1819, when the Boulak printing press was created. It became the official Egyptian printing press and published hundreds of thousands of books on various fields of knowledge.

Textbooks constitute an age-old and original education strategy in Egypt and in the Arab and Islamic world. Each man of knowledge compiled a book which was later used for classes and was commented on by his students and disciples, who added definitions and comments according to the importance of the content and the author of the book. The books were re-edited in a longer or simplified edition and were assigned to the syllabus of the first stage of education. According to the student's development and the academic level, books would gradually be changed from more simplified editions to more detailed and complex editions.

ASFEC, as previously mentioned, was the first to produce a series of textbooks for neo-literates. Subjects include economic, cultural, health and entertainment topics. A special print-type was used to facilitate reading for neo-literates, who will gradually be able to read the printed letters of any book. Many establishments still use the books and they are in wide demand among readers. The same method of large print was used for books on trades and skills for neo-literates. ASFEC also trains experts who write follow-up books concerning skills for use in specialized seminars.

Supplementary and Follow-up Reading Materials

The Ministry of Education published a series of small low-cost books which cover a wide range of subjects. The Ministry had previously published a series of a thousand books. Since the creation of a special organization for books, a yearly book fair is organized in Cairo, Alexandria, and certain governorates, thus allowing neo-literates to purchase books at their own convenience. Recently this organization drew up a plan to publish a thousand books at a low price, based on the old project of the Ministry of Education, so as to provide reading material for continuing education. Certain publishing houses and press organizations have published simple books and periodicals on different subjects such as *The Cultural Library*, published by the General Book Organization, or the series *Your Book*, published by Dar El Maaref, in addition to other periodicals.

There are also magazines in the same field, including the magazine *Youth and the Future Sciences*, published by Al Ahram, *Your Private Doctor*, and many other magazines in a simplified style covering different subjects. Moreover, the Cultural Labour Association publishes simplified magazines and books for the working public.

Libraries and Museums

The Egyptian General Book Organization opened libraries in different parts of Egypt in order to give readers convenient access to books. Mobile libraries are also being implemented by the organization. For the time being they are only being implemented in Cairo but will later be available throughout Egypt. ASFC's role with regard to rural and mobile libraries has already been mentioned. Egypt has a number of museums, which are considered a source of education in terms of the objects on exhibit and the written comments. The museums include the Egyptian Museum, Science Museum, Health Museum, Agriculture Museum and many more. Currently a Natural History Museum is about to be built with the co-operation of Unesco.

Extension Literature Produced by the Development Agencies

Many institutions in Egypt publish simplified publications and pamphlets which provide information about the organization and which are adapted to neo-literates as a complement

to what they have learned previously concerning the process of
the development of society for the purpose of improving the
quality of life in Egypt. Among these institutions is the General Administration for Agricultural Guidance, which is affiliated with the Ministry of Agriculture as well as with the
Council for Rural Information. The General Administration, together with the Council, publishes many pamphlets on agricultural mechanization and on the best methods for cultivating the
main crops in Egypt, as well as new crops which have proved
productive. These pamphlets are generally small and simplified
with colour illustrations. The General Administration for
Agriculture Guidance also publishes a magazine entitled *Agriculture Guidance*, which is distributed to farmers through
agriculture guidance offices and agriculture co-operative societies. Apart from subjects dealing specifically with the
introduction of agricultural practices, the magazine covers a
variety of subjects such as parasites and methods for their
eradication, the food industry, pollution, mechanization, etc.
The magazine's editors simplify the language used and avoid
complicated terms yet generally use the terminology commonly
used by farmers. Posters are also used.

Numerous booklets for health education have been published by the Ministry of Health through the General Administration for Health Education. The booklets deal with preventive
methods for certain widespread illness such as bilharzia and
parasite viruses. They are also concerned with promoting the
principles and methods of general hygiene and discussing illnesses, like dehydration, which children suffer from in summer-
time, ophthalmic infections, care for pregnant women and the
importance of correct methods of nutrition. The booklets also
concentrate on fighting certain social illnesses such as drug
addiction and cigarette smoking. The Ministry of Health also
publishes literature to inform the public on the services provided by health units, family planning and childcare centres
and quarantine units; on how to benefit from these services; on
the procedures to follow to obtain a health card, etc. The
Higher Population and Family Planning Council plays a vital role
by publishing booklets, publications and posters demonstrating
the importance of family planning, the methods it uses and the
effects of overpopulation upon each individual and upon the
process of development of society as a whole.

The Ministry of Social Affairs has also contributed to
these endeavours through its widespread social units. Likewise,
the Ministry of Culture and the Ministry of Information, with

their respective services play a fundamental role in providing citizens with general, national and political guidance, which will be discussed in detail. Each of these organizations holds seminars and arranges training programmes, working sessions and a variety of activities to help citizens continue their education. Mosques and churches also contribute to this cultural movement, especially in the area of religious culture.

Parallel Education

The State offers education opportunities through one-class schools for drop-outs and those deprived of a primary education. It has also provided opportunities to sit for school exams without the requirement of attending formal classes, in addition to allowing evening schools to be opened for the intermediate and secondary stages. These allow students, through affiliation with certain university faculties, to sit for exams; all that is required of students who wish to transfer to formal education is to pass exams with good grades.

The Institute for Commercial Co-operation and the Institute for Agricultural Co-operation are supervised by the Ministry of Higher Education. Both open their doors to workers with a secondary commercial or agricultural certificate who wish to attend evening courses for four years and obtain a degree equivalent to a university first level. The same is offered by the Institute for Productive Sufficiency, which was created at the University of Zagazig.

The Armed Forces have contributed by creating the Tahrir Schools for officers, soldiers and volunteers to enable them to pursue their education and obtain formal education certificates such as the certificate of basic education or the secondary certificate. Channels have been opened between literacy classes and these schools to allow those who have received the literacy certificate to attend these schools, which are located in many military areas. The Ministry of Education has approved and financed their construction since 1981-1982. Ten intermediate and secondary schools have been built (second cycle of basic education) in addition to fifty primary schools (first cycle of basic education) throughout Egypt. The Ministry of the Armed Forces, in co-operation with the Ministry of Education, supervises and supports these schools.

Occasional Programmes

The most important are the rapid training programmes prepared by the Labour Force Organization, which aim at helping neo-literates acquire skills that will allow them to find convenient work. These programmes are organized according to labour requirements and regional circumstances. Programmes are followed up by gradual training to raise the skills and level of performance.

The Ministry of Social Affairs participated in offering occasional programmes for adults in various subjects; the main programmes are aimed at raising the cultural and economic level of women. The Workers' Education Association offers occasional seminars at its centres or in factories to raise workers' cultural, economic and social level. Similarly, the Nile Centres affiliated with the Ministry of Information offer various programmes and seminars to meet the requirements of different groups and keep them up to date on current events.

Radio and Television

Special networks have been designated for the various groups of the population such as workers, farmers and women, and a special network has been designated for youth. A special local radio network has been created, which will be discussed in further detail. Television also offers different specialized programmes for the various population groups, along with educational programmes.

Traditional and Folk Media

By creating the popular university, the Ministry of Education indicated its concern for these media, which provide the opportunity to enrol in classes along with vocational training programmes and education through music, theatre and other popular activities. This developed into a major part of the Ministry of Culture known as the Department of Public Culture, whose centres promote education through popular theatre, cultural debates, etc. Centres are located throughout Egypt.

Sports and Physical Education

The Higher Local Youth and Sports Council plays an important role in physical education through its centres and sport clubs, which exist in many parts of the country. The centres and clubs offer possibilities for physical development, as well as the development of sports skills, and organizes cultural programmes to occupy leisure time.

Vocational Training

Vocational training is the concern of many ministries and organizations such as the Ministry of Education, the Ministry of the Labour Force, the Ministry of Housing, the Ministry of Building and Construction, the Armed Forces, the Ministry of Social Affairs, and others. They offer different programmes for vocational training in various skills for neo-literates, drop-outs from the primary stage, and persons who ended the primary stage or the intermediate stage or who even failed to obtain a certificate. The programmes aim at providing a skill, in addition to general, national and social cultural training, which enables the individual to participate in social and economic activities.

The Ministry of Industry has largely contributed in this field by offering numerous programmes, including:

Programmes for Industrial Apprenticeship

It is one of the most important vocational training programmes in Egypt, where youths receive training in local productive factories until they obtain the basic skills of the vocation. The study period of this programme is three years. The first year specializes in fundamental training, which includes both practical training and theoretical education. The two remaining years concentrate on practical training in industrial companies in which trainees become familiar with the work atmosphere in workshops and factories and acquire expertise from older workers. Training is offered in metallurgy, electronics and precision instruments, chemicals, minerals, printing, weaving and textiles, and the glass and leather industries.

The group most receptive to this programme consists of youths aged 15 to 19. On completion of the programme, contracts are concluded between the youths and the company. A selection is made at the end of the course and a vocational training certificate is granted.

Quick Training Programme

The Ministry of Industry offers these programmes to meet the requirements of many factory and production workers.

The Administration for Production Efficiency and Vocational Training, affiliated with the Ministry of Industry, manages and supervises these programmes, which aim at providing rapid training opportunities to newly appointed workers in different production establishments. This is done to provide vocational qualification for the skills they are expected to perform, in addition to retraining for workers in these enterprises so as to raise their vocational skills.

There are forty-four training centres throughout the country which offer training in various skills such as electricity, mechanics, printing, textiles, precision instruments, tanning, metallurgy, glass, etc.

Programmes Aimed at Improving the Technical Level

These programmes aim at improving the technical level of workers and supervisors in factories through training programmes designed to modernize a vocation or function. Reading and writing are the two conditions required for this programme, along with training experience. The duration of this programme is ten weeks.

The Ministry of Social Affairs contributes in this field with the adult programmes it occasionally offers in different subjects to raise the cultural and economic level of women. Among the main programmes is the productive community project, which provides beginners of both sexes, all ages and of differing educational backgrounds vocational training in different job areas and types of skills before they enter the productive community project. This project began in 1967 with the assistance of UNICEF. Centres are located throughout Egypt and, according to a 1983 report presented by the Ministry of Social Affairs to the Higher Council for Adult and Literacy Education, there are 2,000 vocational training centres in Egypt attended by 26,500 male and female trainees in different vocations such as car mechanics, plumbing, welding, carpentry, electricity, leather tanning, hand-weaving, carpets and rugs, shoemaking, etc.

A training programme on the operation of irrigation

stations, machines and agricultural equipment was organized by the General Organization for Land Reform. The programme also offers training in driving farm tractors and aims at providing learners with the necessary information to operate and ensure the maintainance and repair of farm equipment.

There are also other programmes offered by the Vocational Training Centres, which are affiliated with the Armed Forces and the Ministry of Labour.

A detailed study of education strategies and methods adopted for the post-literacy stages is provided in the following section.

5.   ANALYTICAL STUDY OF SELECTED LEARNING STRATEGIES
      IN EGYPT

5.1   The One-class School for Continuing Education

       General Framework

       New methods of education are being studied in order to
achieve full enrolment of children aged 6 to 8 and to limit
drop-outs from the primary school, thereby eliminating one of
the sources of illiteracy, as well as dealing with the problem
of relapses into illiteracy. These new methods also aim at fulfilling pressing education requirements without creating a
heavy financial burden, and at ensuring adaptation to demographic, social and economic circumstances.

       Therefore, the one- and two-class schools were the form
of implementation agreed upon. They reflect an old education
tradition in Egypt, the 'Kuttab', widespread in cities and villages. The Kuttab was a private institution supervised by the
Ministry of Education. These schools were located in one building, and teaching was performed by a schoolmaster and a reciter
of the Koran who had good knowledge of religion, reading, writing and arithmetic, along with teaching ability and a good re-
putation. One of the advanced, bright pupils was selected to
assist the schoolmaster and was known as 'Al Arif'. Education
in the Kuttab involved learning the Koran by rote, reading,
writing, arithmetic and calligraphy. It is noteworthy that
children were entirely free to attend or leave the Kuttab, no
restriction with regard to age or sex was imposed for enrolment
and the school was open all day. The channels between the
Kuttab and the Azhar University were opened for continuing edu-

cation leading to higher degrees, and channels were also opened between formal education in primary schools and other schools which existed at the time. Education in the Kuttab had no defined period or duration; it ended once the entire Koran had been studied and once the basic skills of reading, writing and arithmetic had been acquired. This was the criterion by which a pupil could be transferred to another establishment of learning.

The one-class school made use of past experience and developed in the field of nonformal education. It became a form of parallel education for all those deprived of an education, and it overcame many obstacles which had led to failures or inattendance by learners. Some basic principles of this type of school are the following:

- Freeing education from the obstacles and formalities which prevent it from spreading in remote areas.

- Facilitating education for deprived groups and adapt schools to the different factors and circumstances of various environments, in accordance with the requirements and conditions of learners.

- Ensuring flexibility with respect to age, educational level, the beginning and end of the academic year and school hours, which may be either in the morning or in the evening, flexibility regarding the curriculum, syllabus and school location.

-ᵢ Creating a strong link between the one-class school and the nearest primary school in order to benefit from its campus, teachers and equipment.

- Opening channels between one-class nonformal schools and formal schools which will permit pupils from the one-class school who have passed their exams to transfer to a formal school. Horizontal transfer is from one cycle to its equivalent class in a formal school, and vertical transfer is from one class to a higher class in a formal school. Learners may thus pursue their education up to the university.

The Ministry of Education drew up a five-year plan in 1975 to create five thousand one-class schools every year for the five years of the plan. The schools would receive 36,000 learners.

Objectives

The one-class school aims at eliminating the sources of illiteracy through:

- Providing education to children aged 6 to 8 who have no formal school in their area.

- Providing educational opportunities for those unable to receive an education when they were between 6 and 8 years of age.

- Providing drop-outs with the opportunity to continue their education before relapsing into illiteracy.

- Developing the individual's culture, knowledge and basic skills which will help him/her continue his/her education and contribute to community activities.

Learners

The system of one-class education aims at providing educational opportunities for the following groups:

- school-age children who failed to enrol in a primary school at the proper time,

- drop-outs who never completed the primary stage,

- learners who have relapsed into illiteracy.

The following table indicates the number of schools during the ten-year period from 1975-1976 to 1984-1985:

Table 7

Number of Schools and Learners in the One-class School

Academic Year	Number of Schools	Number of Learners	Average Attendance
1975-1976	468	25 899	55
1976-1977	1 434	47 722	33
1977-1978	1 845	61 267	33
1978-1979	2 212	61 313	28
1979-1980	2 521	66 333	26
1980-1981	2 376	63 652	27
1981-1982	2 277	60 575	27
1982-1983	2 276	68 358	30
1983-1984	1 705	45 828	27
1984-1985	1 373	37 599	27

The table indicates the following:

- There is significant receptivity on the part of learners to enrol in schools as reflected by the enrolment figures, which are higher than expected, except for the first year.

- Enrolment over the ten years was adequate since it was accompanied by high attendance rates when the schools were opened, with 31 learners in each class, except for the first year of the plan when the average was 55 learners per class as a result of a lack of preparation by the schools.

Learners were aged 6 to 15. The following table indicates the number of learners in the one-class school during the academic year 1984-1985 according to age group.

Table 8

Number of Learners in One-class Schools

according to Age Group during the Academic Year 1984-1985

Age Group	Number of Learners	Percentage
6- 8	14 413	38.3
8-10	10 195	27.1
10-12	7 282	19.4
12-14	4 585	12.2
14 and older	1 124	3.0
TOTAL	37 599	100%

The table indicates the following:

- Approximately one-third of the learners are school-age children between 6 and 8 years of age at a rate of 38.3%.

- Almost half the learners (46.5%) are aged 8 to 12. They are too old to be admitted to the first grade of the basic education stage. Thus, they are given a second chance.

- Only 15.2% of all learners are between 12 an 14 years of age or older. This age group corresponds to the second cycle of basic education (previously the intermediate stage). This group comprises drop-outs from the primary stage who are given another opportunity to receive an education.

These findings are much the same as those from a 1981 study by the National Council for Education and Scientific and Technological Research which indicated that learners between 6 and 8 years of age accounted for 37% of all learners, in a range of as much as 50% in overpopulated governorates and to as low as 10% in the coastline governorates. Children aged 10 to 12 years are the most receptive group for education.

Curriculum and Teaching Methods

The curriculum used in these schools is characterized by flexibility in planning and implementation. In planning, it considers the different education requirements of learners and adapts them to their level, to the level of teachers and to the duration of learning. As for implementation, it considers the relationship to the school's local environment, as well as the subjects of religious, national and social concern to learners. Flexibility is also observed in defining the learning period for the convenience of learners.

The one-class school curriculum includes religious education, learning the Koran, the Arabic language, arithmetic, scientific and health studies and vocational training. The distribution of subjects is as follows:

Table 9

Distribution of Academic Subjects in the One-class School

Subject	No. of hours per week
Religious education	4
Arabic language	6
Arithmetic	4
Social studies	1
Scientific and health studies	1
Vocational training (third grade)	2
Total per week	18

The one-class school is open three hours daily five days a week.

The group method is adopted for teaching, in which learners are divided into groups according to their educational level. Each group has an objective assigned to it which must be fulfilled within a specified period of time. Learners are divided into groups according to their education level as follows:

- a group of full illiterates (first level)

    This group includes illiterate pupils who never enroled in a primary school. The curriculum assigned to this group is designed to achieve a level equivalent to the second primary grade.

- a group of those who have acquired the basic skills of reading and writing (second level)

    This group includes pupils who have acquired the basic skills of reading and writing and who have previously enrolled in primary education but were drop-outs. The curriculum assigned to this group is designed to enable pupils to attain a level equivalent to the fourth primary grade.

- a group able to read, write and solve arithmetic problems (third level)

   This group is comprised of drop-outs from the fourth primary grade or later who read and write well. The curriculum assigned to this group is designed to achieve a level approximately equivalent to the sixth primary grade.

Learners are divided into groups on the basis of an oral and written test which determines the learner's level.

Teachers normally test learners about two weeks after they begin the course so as to determine their level. In many cases two groups or two levels are put together in the same classroom and the teachers divide work among them.

However, the teaching methods used in the one-class school differ from one governorate to another. Once teachers understand the concept and objectives of this school, its role and mission, the differences disappear.

No specific book or syllabus exist for one-class schools, which often use primary stage books.

Employees in One-class Schools

Employees in one-class schools comprise teachers and supervisors.

Teachers

There are three levels of teachers for this type of school:

- First level: This level includes qualified, experienced teachers from nearby primary schools and retired teachers.

- Second level: This level includes employees and educated citizens who wish to teach in a one-class school.

These teachers are faced with certain professional difficulties concerning some of the subjects they teach, therefore training is required.

- Third level: This level includes a large number of Koran instructors, mosque imams and others concerned with certain subjects such as reading, writing and the Koran.

Employment in these schools is short-term, and most of the qualified staff regard it as a temporary job until they find permanent employment elsewhere.

The following table indicates the type of teachers working in these schools and the proportion of each out of a total of 1,340 teachers, according to 1977 Ministry of Education statistics.

Table 10

Type and Percentage of Teachers in the One-class School

Original Vocation	Percentage
Teacher	29.6%
Koran memorizer	25.0%
Employee	21.7%
Imam from a mosque	7.0%
Official performing civil marriages	4.5%
Civil servant	2.4%
Retired teacher	1.4%
Other	8.4%

Some provinces hold training programmes for teachers before they enter one-class schools since learners require special, individual attention. Teachers also require training in selecting groups, following up on the learner's progress and in acquiring the skills needed to work in these schools.

Supervisors

One-class schools are usually created near a formal school, regarded as the mother school, which manages and supervises it under the guidance of a headmaster.

Every governorate appoints a department head to super-

vise these schools, and a department guide undertakes guidance
and follow-up. In certain governorates this function is assigned to adult education guides and in others to special
guides for these schools.

Location of Schools and Their Geographical Distribution

In 1984-85, a total of 1,373 schools were recorded in
twenty-four governorates. The locations for schools are planned,
with priority given to the following:

- sparsely populated small villages, hamlets and
  Bedouin areas,

- villages, districts and populated regions where classes face the difficulty of not being able to receive
  school-age children,

- areas where there are no schools.

The report prepared by the National Research Centre for
Education in 1981 indicates that 37% of these schools function
in buildings which house formal schools, 53% in mosques, 10%
in huts, 12% in a single room and 5% in two rooms; 78% of these
schools have no running water and 75% have no electricity.

Learning Period and Granting of Certificates

Since channels are open between formal and nonformal
education in these schools, the pupils are able to transfer
to a primary school once they have reached a specific level of
education in the one-class school and have passed their second
and fourth grade or the primary certificate examinations.

The period of education is three years, covering the
three above-mentioned grades; at the end of the three years a
certificate is granted and learners may sit for the basic stage
primary cycle examinations.

Fees and Financing

The Ministry of Education finances these schools and no
fees are charged to learners.

5.2   Training Centres for the Building and Construction
        Industry Affiliated with the Ministry of Housing

General Framework

Many departments affiliated with certain ministries,
organizations and public establishments, especially the Ministry of Education, are involved in vocational training programmes in Egypt. The Ministry of Education co-operates with
many other organizations in the public sector to create vocational training centres and organize vocational and skill
training programmes. Some of the organizations offering this
type of training are the Ministry of Industry, the Ministry of
Housing, Construction and Land Reclamation, the Ministry of
Communications, the Ministry of Defence, the Ministry of Social
Affairs and the Ministry of the Labour Force.

It is difficult to define the programmes, activities,
methods and learning strategies used in this field, as it is
difficult to define the target groups which benefit from them.
However, we shall analyse a specific example of the learning
strategy in this field of vocational training within the framework of the endeavours of the Ministry of Housing to provide
trained labour for building and construction, in connection
with the post-literacy education stage.

There is an evident need for additional manpower since
building and construction has expanded in Egypt after the 1973
October War; new cities are being built and others are being
rebuilt. In 1975 the Department of Training for Building and
Construction was created to train the labour force in various
skills related to construction and also to face the deficiency
of skilled labour and to raise the level of workers.

Objectives

- Provide a trained labour force for the building and
  construction industry.

- Supply a type of vocational training for drop-outs
  from primary education, offering them a skill in building and construction which is in demand in the employment market and which will help increase their income.
  Training for this industry requires technical and theoretical study which helps keep learners from relapsing into illiteracy.

The Organization of Training for Building and Construction has prepared special programmes related to different skills,
with units of gradually increasing difficulty.

The education programme includes the following:

- study of the tools and equipment related to the
  industry,

- understanding of the materials involved,

- knowledge of the technical terminology used,

- fieldwork,

- knowledge of unit measures, measurement equipment
  and elementary geometry needed for the work,

- development of the learner's skills in reading,
  writing and oral expression,

- development of the basic forms of arithmetic (addition,
  substraction, multiplication and division) which are
  used for measuring and estimating profits and, in particular, development of a correct and scientific method
  of thinking,

- interest in cultural, historical, social, religious
  and national issues.

Learners in the centres are trained in the following
skills: construction, whitewashing, painting, carpentry, smith-
ing, sanitary work, electrical installation, metallurgy and
flagging.

It should be noted that certain centres offer only some
of all these skills, whereas the number of skills offered in
different centres varies between 3 and 10 according to the size
of the centre, the public concerned and the special equipment
used.

The Regional Centre for Adult Education, ASFEC, in co-
operation with the Organization of Training for Building and
Construction, contributed to preliminary studies and planning
for the construction of the centre in Sirs Al Layan. This
centre therefore differs from others in Egypt, in that it prepares educational materials and training adapted to the

learner's vocational education, culture and aptitude.

ASFEC prepared two series of follow-up books for the building and construction training centres which treat aspects of vocational, religious, historical, cultural, labour and health education. The first series published was entitled *Sanitary Works*, and the second, *The Cultural Book*. The first series was published in three volumes and in preparing these books the following points were taken into consideration:

Content:

- The use of simple, classical Arabic and a style to facilitate understanding by the learner, whose level is the equivalent of the fifth primary grade.

- Exactitude in terms of technical material and scientific content.

- Clarity of meaning, simplicity of language and appropriate book structure.

- The basic scientific terminology used in the vocation, with the Arabic equivalent wherever possible.

- Presentation of ideas in a simple form suited to vocational education.

- Ensure complementarity between the subject and the scientific theories in each book.

- Prepare books by vocation, divided into sequences according to each practical activity, and, eventually, by paragraph or sentence. This facilitates understanding by learners.

- Use a dissertation style in connection with practical exercises.

Composition:

- Gradually modify the print type of the books from large to small type in order to help neo-literates read, then gradually accustom them to regular print type.

- Vary the illustrations and photographs of the books so as to encompass different sectors. The texts are simplified but respect scientific exactness. Colours were not used in every book.

- A set of questions at the end of each book aims at reinforcing the learner's understanding of the practical, theoretical and mathematical training he has received and which will determine his level. The last book of the series concludes with a comprehensive test.

- The series of books includes a *Teacher's Guide* outlining objectives, concepts and method of use.

The books in the series include the following subjects:

- Tools and equipment
- Pipes
- Mortars, materials and pillars
- Valves, plugcocks and taps
- Siphons
- Sanitation equipment
- Sewage
- Mathematics
- Certain elementary scientific theories related to the sanitation industry.

The same principles of education and language apply to the second series of books entitled *The Cultural Book*, published in four volumes in the form of education units, each covering a specific subject.

Unit One: *Work as an Act of Faith*

This unit aims at offering learners an insight into religions, especially the concept of work in Islam and its stress on the love of work, the high degree of respect it deserves, loyalty to work, etc. This unit also covers the ethics of interaction between workers and employers.

It includes the following subjects:

- Work as an act of faith
- Loyalty
- Exactitude in work
- Allah is the provider

- Honesty
- Moderation in spending
- Economy is one half of livelihood
- Cleanliness and hygiene are a part of faith
- Co-operation.

Unit Two: *Building and Construction in Egypt*

This unit covers the historical evolution and stages of building and construction in Egypt since the time of the Pharaohs, and later the Islamic period up to the advent of modern Egypt from the rule of Mohamed Aly to the present time. It aims at teaching learners about the art and creativity of Egyptian architecture and its historical development so as to inspire trainees to perpetuate building and construction activities in contemporary Egypt.

It includes the following subjects:

- The Pyramids
- The Mosque of Amr Ibn Al'As
- The Mosque of Ahmed Ibn Tulun
- The Azhar Mosque
- The barrages
- The High Dam.

Unit Three: *Worker and Society*

This unit aims at acquainting learners with their society, reinforcing a positive attitude towards duties and informing them of their political, civil and trade union rights.

The following subjects are included in this unit:

- The emergence of trade unions
- The functions of the trade unions
- Methods of forming a trade union
- The duties of workers
- Workers' rights
- Our small family.
- Our large family.

Unit Four: *Health is the Worker's Capital*

This unit aims at informing learners of the basics of a worker's general health with regard to nutrition, recreation, industrial security and physical education. It sheds light on the dangers of drugs, alcohol, local diseases and the effects of vocational illnesses on health and productivity.

This unit includes the following subjects:

- Man
- The skeleton
- The digestive system
- The muscular system
- The respiratory system
- The circulatory system
- Nutrition
- Good habits for healthy nutrition
- The components of the human body

Learning Period

The learning period at the centres is six months, divided into four months in the centres and two months in field training under the supervision of an accredited contractor.

The Administration, Organization, and Training Staff

The Organization of Training for Building and Construction, affiliated with the Ministry of Housing and Construction, supervises these centres in every part of the country and, in co-operation with the Ministry of Education, benefits from the industrial secondary schools of certain governorates for use in training. All training programmes are financed by the Organization.

Most of the trainers hold industrial secondary certificates or a diploma from a higher technical institute. They complete training courses either in Egypt or abroad prior to working in the centres.

Granting of Certificates

Learners must sit for an examination at the end of the course before obtaining a certificate from the centre and must present the certificate received from the contractor to prove that they have completed the two months of field training and acquired the skills and ethics of the vocation. The certificate must be approved by the Ministry of Education.

Incentives and Benefits

Learners are offered the following incentives and benefits:

- a food allowance;

- a set of tools and equipment for the vocation training;

- a grant of two hundred pounds for the duration of the course. No fees or expenses are charged to the learner.

5.3   General Culture Programmes

General Framework

The general culture programmes in Egypt aim at developing the individual's maturity using the following method:

- Provide everyone with information and knowledge related to general culture.

- Transmit the experiences and expertise of others in farming, medecine, industry, communications and other aspects of modern life.

- Contribute to literacy and post-literacy programmes by presenting a number of convenient programmes for illiterates, neo-literates and others.

- Strengthen formal education programmes.

These programmes use education strategies and depend primarily on modern media for communication, whereas other programmes rely on a combination of modern and traditional media.

As we are living in a period of popular education, modern media can reach people of all ages, in all locations and at a variety of times. The general cultural programmes use a number of learning strategies and mainly rely on modern media such as radio, cinema or television and at times combine the three. Other modern strategies of education are debates, seminars, theatre, public libraries, etc.

Three media are used for these strategies in favour of public culture, namely:

- television and radio,

- the state information service,

- popular culture.

The role of these media and the education strategies are the following:

Radio

The official Egyptian radio began broadcasting in 1934, more than half a century ago. Before that date radio was privately owned. With the electrification of rural areas, radio spread widely throughout Egypt and radio broadcasting covered every part of the country. The number of listeners is currently estimated at 24.5 million according to the research conducted by the Union of Radio and Television. The main network (the general programme) broadcasts 24 hours a day.

There are two strategies used by Egyptian radio, educational programmes and local radio.

Educational Programmes

Radio offers three types of education programmes:

- Programmes to strengthen formal education: These programmes are broadcast during the academic year for students in different stages and types of education. The programmes are broadcast at set times. It is noteworthy that the weekly magazine *Radio and Television* publishes the texts of the lessons broadcast during the week, thereby combining the written word with the spoken word. The university syllabus is also broadcast for Alexandria University students and other students through the "University on the Air" programme. These programmes are also useful for educated

listeners who wish to continue their education or simply add to their knowledge.

- The literacy programme: The literacy programme went on
the air in 1968. A propaganda campaign against the
danger of illiteracy was launched by the radio prior
to the project to recruit the largest number of educated males and females possible to help educate those
who had not had the opportunity to receive an education. Sixteen years later, in 1984, the programme was
broadcast again.

- Post-literacy programmes: Radio broadcasts include a
large number and variety of programmes aimed at neo-
literates and designed to inform them on simple facts
in different fields. The following outlines a few programmes:

 - "One Minute Please":

 A daily programme broadcast for one minute giving
 tidbits of general knowledge.

 - "The Philosopher Said":

 A daily five-minute programme which uses dialogue to
 present the concepts of virtue and beauty, reinforced
 by Arab and Islamic traditions. This programme has
 been broadcast for almost fifteen years now.

 - "Visiting Someone's Library":

 A weekly one-hour programme which reviews a book or
 books in someone's library and discusses the guest's
 reading interests, habits, the number of books in
 his/her library , how the library was formed, etc.
 This programme arouses the listener's curiosity and
 encourages reading.

 - "Reading for You":

 This programme reviews new books in different fields.

 - "The Political Dictionary":

 This programme discusses certain political concepts

and links them with current national and international events.

- "Our Beautiful Language":

A daily 10-minute-programme on Arabic literature, which uses a simplified method, for example poetry and prose. This programme has been on the air for almost eight years.

- "English for You":

This is an example of the programmes offered in the slot for foreign languages.

- "Five minutes for Your Health":

A five-minute programme broadcast daily to enlighten listeners on proper health and nutrition habits.

Local Radio

The Egyptian Radio created a network of local radios in 1954 aimed at the development of local communities and designed to point out the characteristics of each region, develop awareness among citizens with respect to their region and its problems, services and utilities, and finally to present a vivid image of the region as well as to reinforce formal and non-formal education and offer education services for all. The local network includes the following six radios:

- Alexandria Radio: Created in 1954 as the first regional station, it is considered the core of the comprehensive project for regional radios designed to promote local development.

- The People's Radio: This radio station, which began in 1959, aims to encourage the working population to participate in development efforts.

The People's Radio adopted a particular format - the very reason for its existence - to address farmers and workers throughout Egypt.

- The Youth and Sports Radio: This radio was created in 1975 for youth of different social and cultural backgrounds.

- Central Delta Radio: It serves a limited, well-organized social and economic community. It offers education and information services and takes account of various agricultural and industrial activities.

- The Larger Cairo Radio: Created in 1981, this radio contributes to resolving people's everyday problems and gives listeners the opportunity to share opinions with the authorities.

- Radio North Sai'd (Upper Egypt): Created in 1983, it is of the same orientation and uses the same method as Central Delta Radio.

Egyptian Television

Egyptian television began transmitting in 1960 and has since spread rapidly throughout Egypt. Educational programmes account for 5.17% of total transmitting hours on both the first and second channels; cultural programmes account for 17.5%. Television offers three levels of educational programmes, in addition to complementary programmes for formal education, namely:

Literacy Programmes: These programmes began as a follow-up to two experiments in 1963/64 and 1964/65. ASFEC contributed to the experiments by providing supervision and furnishing the appropriate education materials. Based on previous experimental results, a special literacy programme began broadcasting in November 1968 in co-operation with many concerned ministries and departments such as the Ministry of Education, the local Administration Organizations, the Socialist Union, the Youth Organization, ASFEC and the Rural Council for Information. These programmes were originally intended for group viewing centres. There are 350 such viewing centres in 18 governorates with an average of 30 learners in each centre apart from other undefined numbers. Literacy programmes are still being presented on television.

ASFEC offers training courses for members of the group viewing centres who are police officers who have taught illiterate soldiers in connection with the television programmes.

116

Post-literacy Programmes: Programmes for neo-literates include:

- "Simplified Science": Seventy 15-minute series of simplified subjects were broadcast in 1983/84 on a weekly basis.

- "Teach Yourself" (teaching different skills): This weekly 15-minute programme teaches skills like foundery work, electricity, carpentry, painting, etc.

- "Economics for Everyone": 39 instalments of five minutes each were broadcast in 1981 three times a week.

- Labour programmes: Labour programmes includes "For Whom the Prize", which is shown for half-an-hour once a week. It is a game-show in which workers from different companies and factories are contestants. The games covers topics in vocational, technical, labour, sports and entertainment fields.

- "The Labour Magazine": A weekly programme on different labour activities, which also covers news and the problems of workers.

There are many other programmes for different groups, including women and the rural population.

Education Programmes: The University on the Air offers a variety of programmes for different cultural levels, including a project for raising the level of first stage teachers and qualifying them for a B.A. or B.Sc. in education. Other programmes include the medical education programme, which keeps new graduates informed on the latest developments, and another programme for learning English and French.

The State Information Service

The State Information Service is the official organ for information in Egypt. It began in 1952 as an administration within the Ministry of National Guidance and acquired autonomy in 1967.

This body collects information on local and international public opinion related to events of interest to the country. Through different media, it provides guidance to the local communities.

At the local level, the State Information Service contributes to post-literacy activities through information programmes which aim to reinforce and intensify national concepts
among the population, to assist development efforts in the
villages and to facilitate communication between the population
and the authorities. Two types of centres are in use:

Internal Information Centres

There are 47 of these centres in governorates of Egypt.
Their purpose is to inform citizens on national problems and
on their rights and duties.

The Nile Centres for Training, Information and Education

The Nile Centres were created in co-operation with the
State Information Service and the West Gernnan Hans Sedle Association. They began in 1978 with the aim of developing information and improving popular means of communication. There are
eight centres in eight governorates offering training courses
which depend upon a free and objective dialogue between participants and lecturers, who are selected from the highest level of
experts, professors and specialists.

The centres are equipped with the most up-to-date audio-
visual equipment, and a video system is used for training
courses and debates.

The centres also contribute to post-literacy education
through training courses for neo-literates in different fields
of development. For example, women's education courses are held
for a period of six to nine days; the only requirements are
that participants know how to read and write and they be at
least 20 years of age. The programmes vary in terms of the
subjects offered: "Women and Development", "Communication and
Development", religious values, family planning, health development, consumer guidance, home economics and the problems of
working women.

The Internal Information Centres and the Nile Centres
use the following education strategies to achieve their goals:

(a) Mobile Information Units:

This strategy uses mobile units for the villages and
remote areas. They house a cinema and a theatre, and

offer lectures. Other ministries and institutions
co-operate on implementation. The aim of the units
is to inform the public on social, political and
economic events. The use of these mobile units involves no set conditions.

(b) Cinema and Viewing Clubs:

The films offered are related to entertainment,
farming advice, health education and industrial
safety.

(c) Debates and Public Lectures.

Popular Culture

Popular culture is regarded as the natural extension of
the popular university, which was founded in the forties. Popular culture is a means of life-long education for all as well
as a cultural and entertainment programme for adults and children throughout the country.

Popular culture is affiliated with the Ministry of
Culture and is divided into three specialised centres:

(a) The Centre for Children's Culture
(b) The Centre for Rural Culture
(c) The Centre for Leadership Training.

There are seven central administrations:

- The Administration for Culture
- Plastic Arts
- The Administration for Libraries
- The Administration for the Theatre and Popular Arts
- The Music Administration
- The Administration for Culture and Programme Caravans
- The Administration for Cultural Clubs and Associations.

Popular culture programmes are organized in cultural
palaces, which are widespread in the capitals of governorates
and large Egyptian cities. There were 33 palaces and 38 cultural clubs in Egyptian villages in 1980.

Popular culture has employed the following learning
strategies:

Public Libraries

Public libraries are widespread in cultural palaces and houses. There are 26 public libraries in different cities. Books on general subjects are available and it is easy for readers to find books adapted to their level of education. The libraries open their doors to all with no restriction.

The collection and selection of books is based on a study regarding the trends and interests of each region or village in which a library is found. The list of books is submitted by the manager of the cultural club to the director of the cultural palace, who in turn submits the demand to the central administration of libraries in Cairo.

A system of lending books, as well as other services, is offered by the libraries in addition to reading contests and debates. Most libraries have no qualified librarians, therefore the central administration provides the necessary training courses in Cairo and ensures the classification of books before they are sent to the cultural clubs in the villages.

Service Classes

These classes aim at contributing to continuing education in a style similar to formal education, although the executive procedure differs. The classes are created in the cultural palaces and clubs and are open to the public without restriction.

Education in these classes combines vocational training and a liberal education, including foreign languages such as English, French, German, Italian and Hebrew, and knitting, sewing, embroidery, home economics, typing and shorthand, secretarial training, wireless and electronics, electricity, mechanics, photography, cinema photography, ceramics, carpet and rug crafts, music, drama, painting, sculpture and engraving.

Mobile Cultural Units

This is one of the main forms of popular culture, with a degree of popularity which facilitates its mission for adult education. The units are equipped with microphones and projectors, and they house libraries. The unit is usually accompanied by singers and musical troups, and also offers puppet shows and folklore art exhibitions.

The mobile cultural units also aim at spreading health awareness and fostering nationalism among citizens. Twenty-one units in various villages serve deprived areas.

6.   CONCLUSION

Egypt has consistently adopted learning strategies for the post-literacy stage thanks to the endeavours of national specialists and experts in this field, and to the efforts made by ASFEC over a period of thirty years. It has also been at the forefront of education with the Ashar University, printing which led to press publications, books and pamphlets, the creation of libraries and museums, language schools and skills training, the popular university as a specific institution for adult education, and finally all the other educational institutions which have been mentioned.

The fundamental problem facing Egypt is the lack of a specialised body to co-ordinate the efforts of different establishments and institutions, which often lead to repetitive programmes. Although the Ministry of Education is regarded as the official body responsible for the co-ordination, the abundance of programmes makes co-ordination an extremely difficult task.

The State has formed for this purpose the Higher Council for Adult and Literacy Education as well as the Higher Population Council.

122

REFERENCES

References in Arabic

1. *Union of Radio and Television. Annual Book 1982/83,* Cairo: Union of Radio and Television, 1983.

2. Ahmed Ezzat Abd El Karim. *The History of Education in Egypt since the Rule of Mohamed Aly until the Early Rule of Tewfik 1948-1882",* Cairo: Ministry of Public Education (D.T.), Part II, (N.D.)

3. ASFEC. *The Proposed Strategy for Literacy Education in the Arab World: The Conclusion and Results of the Study.* Sirs Al Layan: ASFEC, 1981.

4. *The Silver Jubilee, 1953-1978.* Sirs Al Layan: ASFEC, 1978.

5. Central Organization for Mobilizing and Statistics. *General Population Statistics: Total of the Republic.* Cairo: Central Organization for Mobilizing and Statistics, 1978.

6. *The Annual Book of the General Statistics of the Arab Republic of Egypt, 1952-1971.* Cairo: Central Organization for Mobilizing and Statistics, July 1972.

7. *The Population of Egypt is 45 Million Persons.* Report issued by the Central Organization for Mobilizing and Statistics in the Population Studies: quarterly publication, 10-64, January/March 1983, pp. 39-50.

8. Abd El Hamid Lotfy and Hassan Al Saaty. *Studies on Demography.* Cairo: Dar Al Maaref, 1981, p.7.

9. Abd Al Satar Al Halongy. *Rural Library Services: Field Study.* Sirs Al Layan: ASFEC, 1979.

10. *Glimpses on the History of Books and Libraries,* Cairo: Dar Al Thagafa for printing and publishing, 1979, p. 2

123

11. Abd Al Fatah Karndil. "Counter-strategy for Overpopulation and Criticism". *The Development Strategy in Egypt: Research and Discussion of the Second Annual Scientific Conference of Egyptian Economists.* Cairo: 24-26 March 1977, The General Book Organization, 1978, pp. 461-496.

12. Karima Karim. "Distribution of Income Between Urbanity and Rurality in Egypt, 1952-1975". In *The Egyptian Economy during a Quarter of a Century, 1952-1977: Analytical Study of the Structural Development Studies and Discussions of the Third Annual Scientific Conference of Egyptian Economists.* Cairo: The Egypt General Book Organization, 23-25 March 1978.

13. Specialised National Councils. *Literacy and Adult Education: Plan and Studies.* Cairo: Specialised National Council, 1977.

14. The Higher Council for Literacy and Adult Education. "Records of sessions since 1982 until April 1985" (photocopy).

15. National Council for Education and Scientific and Technological Research. "Report Presented by the President of the Republic on the Work of the Council During its Fifth Session, October/July 1977-1978." Cairo: Specialised National Council, 1978.

16. Mohamed Mahmoud Radwan. "Literacy and Adult Education in Egypt. Towards a Comprehensive National Plan." Cairo, 1975 (photocopy).

17. Mahmoud Rushady Khater. Literacy Campaign in Certain Arab Countries. Sirs Al Layan: ASFEC, 1960.

18. Mahmoud Al Kurdy. *Civilizationary Development: A Study on the Phenomena of Urban Polarization in Egypt.* Cairo: Dar Al Maaref, 1977.

19. National Centre for Education Research and the International Bank. *Informal Education During the First Level in Egypt: the Primary Sectional Survey Study.* Cairo: April 1981 (photocopy).

124

20. State Information Service. *Egypt in Facts and Data*. Cairo: State Information Service, 1985.

21. Ministry of Education. *Development and Modernization of Education in Egypt: Its Policy, Plans and Realization Programmes*. Cairo: Ministry of Education, July 1980.

22. *Education Policy in Egypt*. Cairo: Ministry of Education, July 1985.

23. Ministry of Education. The General Administration of Statistics and Computer. *Stationary Statistics of the Different Education Stages in 1984/85 According to the Situation as from 15 November 1984*. Cairo: Ministry of Education, 1985.

24. General Administration for Primary Education *Memorandum of the One- or Two-class School Experiment since 1975-1976 until 1984-1985*. Cairo: Ministry of Education, 1985 (photocopy).

25. Office of the Undersecretary of the Ministry of Primary Education, *Working Paper Regarding the one- or two-class School*. Cairo: Ministry of Education, 1975 (photocopy).

References in English

1. Galal, Abdel Fattah. "Urbanization in Egypt and its Implication for Education, 1900-1960." Unpublished M.A. thesis submitted to the Institute of Education, University of London, 1963.

2. Galal, Abdel Fattah. "Adult Education in the U.A.R. (Egypt) with Special Reference to the Work of Selected Organizations." Unpublished Ph.D. thesis submitted to the Institute of Education, University of London, 1966.

3. Ministry of Industry, P.V.T. Dept. "Vocational Training: Apprenticeship System, Accelerated Training System and Upgrading System". Cairo: P.V.T. Dept., (N.D.).

Chapter 3

DEVELOPMENT OF LEARNING STRATEGIES
FOR LITERACY, POST-LITERACY AND
CONTINUING EDUCATION IN KUWAIT

by

Yacoub Al-Sharah
and
Deeb Khabbas

1. INTRODUCTION

The objective of this study is to shed light on the development and progress of the literacy and adult education policy
in Kuwait. The policy is based on the concept of continuing education while indicating the actual relationship between the
public education system on the one hand and literacy and adult
education on the other. It thus indicates the integration, parallelism and differences that exist between them.

This study is also the result of a request formulated by
the International UNESCO Institute for Education, Hamburg. It
is part of a comprehensive study undertaken by this institute
within the framework of lifelong education on the development
of learning strategies for post-literacy and continuing education in Arab countries. Kuwait is in the vanguard as a result
of its expertise and efforts undertaken in this field.

In order to carry out the aims of this study, it is necessary to take into consideration the social, political, economic
and cultural background of each country involved. While the
existing parallels and differences between them are natural, the
education policies, through this interaction, will influence the
general strategy as will be clarified further.

The aims of the general education policy in Kuwait are as
follows: "Adequate opportunities are to be offered to the people
to develop the maximum integral and comprehensive moral, spiritual, intellectual, social and physical potentials of the Kuwaiti
society according to its objectives and ideology derived from
the principles of Islam and Arab contemporary culture. This
should create a balance between individual self-realization and
a constructive participation in the progress of the country in
particular and the Arab and international community in general."
(1)

This general notion and goal stem from the Kuwaiti insight
that human resources are a major source of wealth. Therefore,

all efforts are being undertaken in order to promote education and to instill in individuals the concept of continuing education, thus giving their lives direction as well as benefiting society. From such a viewpoint the community as well as the country and humanity at large will benefit and progress.

Evolution and change are inherent in educational strategy due to revisions and alternatives, yet a permanent basis of motivation is important to maintain, i.e., "the education of the individual and the assistance in enabling him or her to continue studies over a lifetime." (2)

2. A GENERAL OVERVIEW OF KUWAIT'S GEOGRAPHIC, DEMOGRAPHIC, ECONOMIC AND EDUCATIONAL SITUATION

2.1 Geographic Situation

Kuwait is considered a natural outlet of the northeast Arab peninsula as a result of its excellent geographic position along with its ancient trade routes linking it to different regions.

It is located in the extreme northwest of the Arab Gulf between latitudes 28 and 30 degrees north, and longitudes 46 and 48 degrees east. Iraq borders Kuwait in the north and east, Saudi Arabia in the south. A 290 kilometre eastern shoreline overlooks the Gulf. Kuwait's surface area totals 17,818 square kilometres.

Climate

Kuwait's general climate is determined by both the desert climate and the Mediterranean climate found in the Gulf region. There are two major seasons: a long hot summer and a short warm winter.

- Winter is from December to February

- Spring is from March to May

- Summer is from June to September

- Autumn is from October to November.

2.2 The Demographic Situation and the Enrolment in General Education

The population base is considered as the primary step for the education process. The 1985 census numbers 1,695,128, of whom only 40.1% are Kuwaiti and 59.9% are non-residents. The

Kuwaiti population growth rate is 3.7% while average population growth rate is estimated at 4.53%. A rate of 99 males per 100 females in a society is considered a stable population growth.

In view of the difference between the resident and non-resident populations, the average enrolment of students in public school general education programmes also differs: 24.7% for non-residents compared with 18.6% for Kuwaitis. Accordingly the total number of general education students during the academic year 1984-1985 was 347,254 of which 17,432 (50.1%) were Kuwaities. The rate of Kuwaiti female students reached approximately 48.9% of total Kuwaiti public education enrolment, thus indicating a lack of social barriers against the education of females and the opportunity for them to participate in future development, since females represent a considerable proportion of the country's human resources.(3)

Number of Schools and the Education Staff for General Education

According to 1984-1985 statistics, Kuwait's 527 schools consist of 78 kindergartens, 183 primary schools, 164 intermediate schools, 94 secondary schools and 8 secondary specialized schools. The teaching staff numbers 24,965 male and female instructors.(4)

The Present Education Structure in Kuwait

The present education structure in Kuwait consists of the following: kindergarten, primary, intermediate, secondary, non-university education, university education and post graduate education.

The types of education within this structure are as follows:

(1) *General education* (a system of academic years in the schools)

(2) *Specific education* comprised of two sectors:

   Government sector including: special education for handicappeds, literacy and adult education, parallel education, religious education and private education following the national scheme.

   Private sector including: foreign schools which are

not subject to rules of general education applied in Kuwait (except for the syllabus of Arabic language and religion which are submitted to the Ministry of Education).

These schools do not benefit from the financial sub-sidies offered by the Ministry. However, certain schools follow the curriculum of the Ministry and are, therefore, granted certain support, whether moral or financial. These schools comprise the following education stages: nursery, kindergarten, primary, inter-mediate and secondary.

(3) *Vocational Education and Training* which include:

(a) Educational institutes for both male and female instructors, Institute of Technology, Institute of Health, Institute of Commerce and Institute of Telecommunications.

(b) Training centres for students who cannot continue their education in general schools. Training programmes qualify them to work in various tech-nical fields and also train employees to improve their qualifications (community service centres).

(4) *University and Post Graduate Education*

There are various faculties of specialization in which students obtain a B.A., M.A. or Ph.D.

(5) *Programmes for Community Services and Continuing Education*

The government sector provides certain programmes at the university, vocational institutes and the Minis-try of Education. The private sector has a large num-ber of private institutes which offer the public a variety of evening education programmes.

Education Budget

According to the Ministry of Planning, the 1984-85 edu-cation budget reached almost 8.2% of the state's budget of 265,205 million dinars. This is indicative of the different forms of expenditures undertaken by the country during the past

twenty-five years as a result of the oil revenues, which encouraged a high development rate and reinforced the economic
structure. This has resulted in a high standard of services
and one of the highest per capita per annum rates in the world:
according to the 1984-85 statistics of the Ministry of Planning, the 1983 per capita per annum reached 4,375 dinars (approx.
US-$ 15,000). (5)

Cost of Adult and Literacy Education

In comparing the average costs per student in adult centres during 1979/1980, 1980/1981 and 1981/1982, we notice an
increase which is evident in the following table:

Table 1

Learner-Oriented Literacy at Different Stages from 1979-1982

Education Stages for Adults	Average cost per learner	Academic year
1 - Literacy Stage	72 dinars 81 " 101 "	1979/1980 1980/1981 1981/1982
2 - Intermediate Stage for Adults	80 dinars 82 " 114 "	1979/1980 1980/1981 1981/1982
3 - Secondary Stage for Adults	79 dinars 84 " 119 "	1979/1980 1980/1981 1981/1982

The table also indicates that the cost per learner in the
literacy stage is less than that for learners in both the intermediate and secondary stages, which are more or less the same.
(6)

*Expansion in the Development Rates and the Increase in
Labour Demand*

The expansion of development has increased the demand for
additional labour to a point which exceeds the quantitative
capacity of the Kuwaiti society, since a modern society requires qualified technical expertise.

Kuwait lacks qualified manpower, particularly in fields requiring manual and technical skills, though not in the supervisory and writing functions that are related to human sciences and literature. The rate of those functions are 57% for the supervisory jobs, 44.3% for bureaucratic jobs and 42.4% for literary and academic functions.

The role of technical and manual skills is being re-evaluated and upgraded to benefit forthcoming generations thanks to the role played by education, but it is presently missing in the national cadres. Adult education may raise the standard of the national labour force by improving the level of education and allowing graduates of literacy programmes and adult centres to advance to more productive skills.

In 1984-85 almost 40,495 persons, or 31.6% of Kuwait's labour force, were employed in ordinary and semi-skilled functions. They are generally illiterate with a very poor level of education, thus adult education will help promote their standard of performance.(7)

The Relation Between Education and Socio-economic Development

To summarize the above-mentioned information, social and economic development depends on two major elements: first, the increase of the national labour force and second, the improvement of productivity. Therefore education and training are the two pillars of development and a guide to improve the productivity and performance of the labour force.

3. SITUATION OF LITERACY AND ADULT EDUCATION IN KUWAIT

3.1 Historical Background

In view of the direct relationship that exists between formal education and literacy and adult education, it is necessary to summarize the process of general education in Kuwait in order to understand all the efforts undertaken in that field. This brief summary intends to present a comprehensive idea of the process while taking into consideration the stages of development and strategies within a time framework that led to the implementation of a special system of literacy and post-literacy education for adults.

Education in Kuwait began in mosques, where an immam taught all the precepts and traditions of the Islamic religion with extra lessons for the teachings of the Prophet, explanation of certain verses of the Koran, tales of Islamic heroism and Arab grammar.

The Koran schools or *kuttabs* were established in 1887 and were the equivalent of today's schools. In the *kuttabs* students studied reading, writing and arithmetic in addition to learning the Koran by rote. They were instructed by a Mulla or a 'Mutawa' who acquired his title and function as a result of this religious knowledge and his ability to persuade people to follow the right path.

Education was limited to mosques and kuttabs until 1912, when the first formal school was established, the Mubarkia School for Boys. The second school was founded in 1921, the Ahmadia School for Boys, and during the academic year 1937/38 two additional schools for boys and one for girls were opened and known as Al Kobla.

Gradually formal schools began to spread. The oil boom accelerated the process since greater possibilities were available and a large annual budget was granted specifically for building and establishing schools, thus creating a new transition in which education no longer relied on domestic or personal efforts, but on the participation of the government, which headed the Administration of Education.

From the start the principles of education were diverse, and in 1941/42 the study of commerce was introduced in the supplementary classes of the Mubarkia school.

In 1947/48 a religious institute was founded and a Ministry of Education was created, in 1953/54 an institute for female instructors was inaugurated and the following year, in 1954/55, a technical school was opened by the state in view of the need for technical education. This development expanded until the University of Kuwait and different technical schools were established.

The educational ladder developed from two stages, the primary and secondary, to three stages: kindergarten, primary and secondary. Presently it has developed to four stages: kindergarten, primary, intermediate and secondary.

Education at the beginning was not limited to any age group. Both young and old could easily and equally join the same class without inhibition since the common goal was the search for knowledge, which was the first link between public education and adult education.

The basis of formal education was created in 1912, prior to that date no defined syllabus or education system existed.

3.2   Evolution of Literacy and Adult Education Work

The work phases in the field of literacy and adult education may be divided as follows:

- Period prior to the organized work between 1950-1958.

- Period of organized work when special centres were opened for literacy and adult education (intermediate-secondary) in 1958-1981.

- Period of compulsory literacy education under Law No. 4 (1981) and the continuation of adult education.

The education revival of the early fifties brought limited efforts for literacy and adult education in Kuwait. The efforts were limited to the personnel working in schools, patients in health centres, workers in the labour cultural centre, police training centres, military camps and a few citizens who enrolled in classes sponsored by the Islamic Guidance Association. The situation remained pretty much the same until 1957. None of the above-mentioned groups could enrol in formal schools due to their age or because of a job. (8)

Beginning of the Organized Efforts for an Education System for Adults in 1957/58

Following the first demographic survey of 1957, steps were initiated towards organizing efforts for literacy education. In 1958 the first two literacy centres for men were authorized, one in the city of Kuwait in the Kathima School and the other in the city of Al Jahraa, in which 350 learners voluntarily enrolled. In 1963 the first two literacy centres for women were opened, with an enrolment of 420 students. (9)

The project began in February 1958 according to an implementation agreement between Education Department and the Department of Social Affairs and Labour.

With the beginning of the academic year 1966/67, the Authority of Literacy and Adult Education was transferred by decree to the Ministry of Education. The planning of projects, their implementation, supervision and follow-up were thus under the Ministry's authority, in addition to the development and expenditures on literacy and adult education projects.

The results of Kuwait's 1957 census point out the increase of efforts for literacy and adult education. The illiteracy rate in the ten-year-old and above age group was very high. (See Table in Appendix 1.)

Table 2
Illiteracy Rates of Over-10 Year Male and Female Population Compared with General Illiteracy Rate (1957)

Total population (1957 census)	General illit-eracy rate	% of Kuwaiti females in the over-10 age group	% of Kuwaiti males in the over-10 age group
107 246	63.3%	91.7%	89.5%

Note: The general rate of illiteracy for Kuwaiti males and females in the 10-year-old and above age group was 90.5%.

The Law Mandating Compulsory Education for the Young

Until 1965 public education was optional and left to the discretion of the parents. This accounts for the high rate of il-literacy among the age group of the ten-year-old and above despite efforts undertaken to encourage literacy among all age groups. Therefore in 1965 a second law made education compulsory for all persons between the ages of seven and sixteen. This law was implemented during the academic year 1966/67 for both boys and girls. Compulsory education in public schools decreased the spread of illiteracy, thus allowing greater concentration on literacy and adult education as well as a post-literacy stage for those who had missed the opportunity or were unable to attend a day school and could not continue their education.(10)

Literacy and Adult Education Projects for Selected Targets During the Period Between 1969 and 1976

These projects were a result of the state's endeavour to expand the field of literacy work outside the centres to accom-modate those who could not join an adult class and desired edu-cation, as well as to implement additional innovative ideas.

Among the projects and experiments is the literacy of employees in state organizations or other sectors. This project includes the following:

(a) *Armed Forces Education Programme*

Two centres were opened for the education of members

of the armed forces in agreement with the Ministry of Defense during the academic year 1969/70.

The Ministry of Education, in co-operation with the head of the military staff, participated in the preparation of tests for those who could read and write in order for them to obtain a literacy certificate enabling them to pursue their education in the intermediate and secondary stages.

(b) *Literacy Campaign for Policemen*

This successful project began in 1967 with the opening of special centres for policemen's literacy education.

(c) *Literacy Project for Taxi Drivers*

This project was initiated by the Ministerial Cabinet in 1974: 280 drivers enrolled for the literacy stage.

(d) *Education Project for Inmates of the Central Prison*

In co-operation with the Ministry of Internal Affairs, a literacy and adult education centre was established during the academic year 1976/77. The centre eventually included all educational levels, i.e. primary, intermediate and secondary, to prepare the learners for a new life upon release.

(e) *Education Project for Juvenile Delinquents*

The Ministry of Education inaugurated in 1977 the Youth Centre for Adult Education, offering literacy courses for juvenile delinquents in confinement. Eventually three education levels were included: primary, intermediate and secondary.

Functional Education

The brick factory was chosen in 1970 as an experimental field for functional education and a means of employing acquired education skills to improve the standard of performance among workers. The experiment was successful and most of the workers achieved literacy and later continued their education at the intermediate stage in an adult centre.

A preliminary study was undertaken in 1971 in co-ordination with the Agriculture Department in the Ministry of Public Works in order to try out functional education among farmers. However, this study did not reach the implementation phase.

Project for Televised Literacy Instruction

A specialized committee was formed in 1976/77 to outline a televised literacy programme as a supplementary form of literacy education. It was to offer the opportunity for all those who could not attend a literacy class to benefit from the projects, in addition to preventing lapses among those who attended the classes. The project of televised instruction would have needed six months of preparation before becoming widespread and comprehensive.

Two of the major obstacles in the implementation of such a project are the high cost and the necessary technical team to set it in motion. For these reasons the project was never realized.

Evaluation of the Projects

In the light of these experiments, literacy programmes were limited to adult centres for the following reasons:

- Close proximity of rural and urban areas

- Literacy and adult education centres for men and women are widespread in all regions of the country

- Plans and books for learners are continuously developed in order to suit the various vocations and age groups

- Expenses are directed in consideration of schools and staff available for adult instruction

- Learners are encouraged to attend the post-literacy stage in the adult classes, which is one of the aims of continuing education.

Efforts have mostly been directed at guiding illiterates of both sexes and of different age groups to join literacy centres. Education programmes are developed, organized, followed up, and modified in a comprehensive and precise manner

140

within a unified syllabus in the centres which encourage students to continue further education.

Major Field Studies Concerning the Problems Facing Literacy Programmes

The Education Subcommittee of the Board of Ministers undertook a comprehensive field study in 1977/78 concerning two factors contributing to illiteracy and the major efforts undertaken to overcome them.

These two factors are the lack of attendance and the reluctance among illiterates to enrol in the classes; when they do, they drop out shortly after.

This study was made with the assistance of the Administration for Adult Education and the University of Kuwait (students from the Sociology Department). Studies have confirmed the need for legislation to guide literacy education.

Controlling Student Attendance

In order to control absenteeism and dropping out, the Ministry appointed a social cultural supervisor for each centre beginning in the academic year 1975/76 to carry out the following:

- Monitor the regularity of student attendance as well as record statistics on the daily and monthly movement of students by category.

- Study the reasons for absenteeism and organize meetings with the students to foster understanding and to help them overcome the obstacles which keep them from attending.

- Undertake follow-up case studies of students who change from public education to the centres.

- Set up field studies concerning students and the education process in order to understand the problems they are faced with. This method has been very successful.

3.3   New Efforts and Trends in the Provision of Literacy and
       Adult Education

The ongoing efforts exerted over the twenty-five years
from 1958 to 1981 for literacy and adult education resulted in
decreasing the illiteracy rate from 63.3% in 1957 to 32.6% in
1980. Illiteracy also decreased in the age group of ten-year-
olds and above from 90.5% in 1957 to 50.7% in 1980. Some
Kuwaitis find this rate of decrease insufficient and unadapted
to the goals of the country. Therefore, rapid measures are
being taken for a comprehensive revival and development of
adult education in the framework of continuing education. With
Law No. 4 in 1981 a new era for compulsory literacy education
was born. A definition of the groups falling under the compulsory law was outlined in the decree of August 8, 1981.(11)

A Higher Committee and a Permanent Committee were formed
in order to implement the law in carrying out the concept of
comprehensive literacy education. The Committees include all
the organizations and sectors involved in literacy education,
together with the main central guide and motivator, i.e. the
Ministry of Education.(12)

Main Objectives of Adult Education in Kuwait

The development of principal objectives in literacy and
adult education, as a specific form of education, may be summarized as follows(13):

- Literacy for male and female individuals in the compulsory age group, as well as others, guaranteeing more
  educational skills at the fourth-grade level of the
  primary public education and accompanied by an official
  literacy certificate.

- Offer all possible opportunities in order to encourage
  adults to continue their post-literacy education and
  not relapse into illiteracy. Fulfill the concept of
  continuing education.

- Supply male and female students at all stages with
  adequate social, health and general knowledge as a
  means of opening new doors for them to apply their
  technical skills and acquire extra knowledge.

- Offer opportunities for adults to improve their education in order to advance their economic, social and moral situation while also improving their functional performance, their participation in child education and their active contribution to the comprehensive development programmes.

- Offer an alternative form of education for formal school pupils who fail and cannot adapt to the school community. With the parents' consent, along with the pupil's desire to change the educational programme, he or she may join an adult centre and continue his or her education under the supervision of a specialized social worker in the centre.

Teaching Methods Employed in Literacy and Adult Education Centres

The teaching methods in general depend on the traditional method for adult education, that is the interaction between student, instructor and the syllabus. This is also the method found in public education schools.

Certain explanatory methods found in public education schools are adopted for the intermediate and secondary stages of adult education, in addition to the use of available equipment and material found in those schools.

Structure and Administration of Literacy and Adult Education

The Administration of Literacy and Adult Education is the central agency for the supervision of all literacy and adult education programmes in the country. The main functions of this agency are the drafting of working plans and an annual budget estimate implementation, supervision, follow-up and development of all the educational operations, in addition to drawing up programmes of literacy and adult education in Kuwait under the supervision of the Ministry of Education. The Administration also sets the rules and objectives of the Comprehensive Education Programme.

The Administration is divided into the following sections which supervise the management and field work:

(a) Supervision of technical services:

- Section divided into branches: one for the exams and the other for student affairs

- Section for social and cultural affairs, with technical guidance for social and cultural activities affiliated with it

- Section for information which is in direct connection with the technical guidance for social and cultural activities.

(b) Supervision of management and financial services:

- Section for management and financial affairs which is divided into two branches: a branch for literacy education and another for adult education. Two other branches include a branch for books and the secretariat, and a branch for legal affairs in the implementation of the literacy law.

(c) Technical guidance for adult education (during the intermediate and secondary stages)

(d) Technical guidance during the literacy stage (specific to literacy)

(e) Secretariat branch.

(See Figure 1: Structure of the Administration of Literacy and Adult Education.)

The Supervisory System in Literacy and Adult Centres

The supervisor is responsible for the implementation of cultural and administrative plans for literacy and adult education. Every centre has a system linked to the administration and its branches which have specific assignments.

Centre supervisor

Supervisors are generally selected from among the headmasters and headmistresses of public education schools. While it is preferable that the supervisor be a headmaster or mistress, if none are available a candidate may be chosen from

144

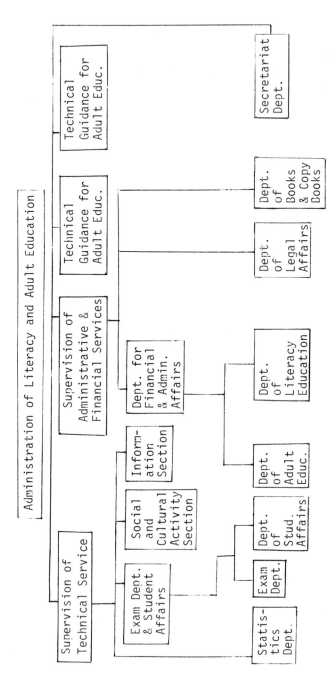

Figure 1: Structure of the Administration of Literacy and Adult Education

the experienced teaching staff. The role of a supervisor is to:

- Supervise the attendance and performance of workers in the centres by implementing the regulations of the administration

- Submit an annual report concerning their work

- Guide and authorize the books, reports and statistics issued by the administration and departments of the centres

- Oversee general supervision of the management of the centres and the relation between learners and instructors

- Establish a close relationship between the centres and the surrounding community by inviting the community members to all the centres' activities.

Technical supervision of the adult education process

The groups supervising the education process in the centres are as follows:

- Technical guides in each centre and in all the stages

- Primary instructors for both the intermediate and secondary stages of adult education.

The role of the *technical guides* is:

- To supervise the implementation of the general technical guiding plans of every subject

- To guide and teach both male and female instructors assigned to the centres in order to guarantee the best methods of education in the centres. This is carried out in the following manner:

    Creating guidance courses at the beginning of each academic year to outline the methods of interaction between instructors and adults, especially newcomers

    Providing technical guidance in the method of teaching the different subjects

- Following up the implementation of field education plans

- Evaluating male and female teaching performance through technical reports at the end of each year

- Contributing to the development of the books and the syllabus for all stages.

As a complement to the administrative aspects, the centre submits an annual report on each instructor which determines his or her reappointment or dismissal. The reports are written according to the performance of the instructor, including his or her degree of patience and tolerance along with the psychological approach towards adults.

Thus adult students are guaranteed all the care and understanding necessary to motivate them to continue their education.

Manager of the centre

The manager is selected from managers of public education schools, especially those who are in schools where adult centres have been created. In case the school manager cannot assume this function, a manager with technical and administrative talents is selected from either the teaching staff or from the school section supervisors.

The functions of the manager are to replace the supervisor in case of absence, supervise the committee for the selection of students at the end of the year and prepare annual statistics on the skills, age, sex and nationality of the students. The manager also follows up the implementation of the daily schedules and supervises the distribution of text books to students in the centre.

Community Cultural Supervisor

This employee is generally selected from the public education social experts affiliated with the social and psychological services of the Ministry and experienced male and female instructors who are ready to work with adults and implement the plans and programmes of the community cultural activities of the centre. The major functions of this position are to:

- Follow up the continuity and attendance of students in the centres, observe the daily continuity movement and organize the necessary records.

- Study each case of absenteeism individually by meeting with the student to find out the reasons and exert the maximum efforts to remove all obstacles.

- Supervise the implementation of the cultural and guidance programmes in the centres.

- Offer assistance in the field and social studies undertaken by the various departments of the Administration.

- Supply the Statistics Department of the Administration on a monthly basis with all the data concerning the numbers and percentages of students and their attendance in all classes.

- Submit monthly and annual reports of his functions in the centre to the Social and Cultural Activity Department of the Administration.

- Resolve conflicts and problems which may arise among students and organize a prize-giving day.

Secretary of the centre

The secretary of the centre is selected from the work force of public education day schools with priority given to those connected with the Office of the Registrar and Student Affairs. His or her functions are the following:

- Handle all incoming and outgoing paper work concerning the centre.

- Register the old and new male and female students in the centre and record the names that were crossed out and returned to the centre.

- Prepare specific statistics concerning skills, age, nationality, dropout rate and re-registration of students.

- Prepare student files, including academic results and progress.

Stock clerk

His or her function is to guard and maintain the centre's equipment, books and tools, which he or she registers in a ledger under the supervision of the manager of the centre. The specifications are sent to the general warehouse.

Science instructors

Science instructors are closely affiliated with the science teachers during the intermediate and secondary stages and therefore included in the teaching budget. There is more than one instructor, depending on the science subject being taught, i.e. geology, chemistry, biology and physics. They are responsible for laboratory equipment and material, as well as for the preparation of the experiments with the assistance of the laboratory teacher.

Data and Statistics Concerning the Present Position of Literacy and Adult Education

In order to understand the present position of this form of education by the end of academic year 1984/85, it is necessary to look into this year's statistics made by the Administration of Literacy and Adult Education (Statistics Department), with particular attention to the following points:

(a) Up to a certain limit, students in adult centres may attend more or less often within a month since adult education is optional, unlike the compulsory literacy stage. When absenteeism exceeds the defined limit, however, students are suspended from the classes and must renew their registration to be readmitted. Statistics constantly vary since those suspended may be re-admitted in addition to new enrolments.

(b) There are two periods during the academic year when a comprehensive survey is undertaken:

- End of October, when student registration is highest.

- April, when student registration is lowest relative to the list of the remaining students.

(c) Some students regularly attend the whole course but

miss the end of the first term tests, which they make up at the end of the second term in September. Therefore the first term results are generally poor compared to the number of graduates at the end of the second term.

By noting the number of students during the two periods, an evaluation of the rate of dropouts and successes for 1984/85 is possible. Thus the situation of adult education can be determined. An example follows (for more details see Appendices 2 and 3):

The number of students registered in the different stages of adult education for the academic year 1984/85 (14):

October 1984:   39,996

April 1985:   31,368

Attending first term
exams in May 1985:   26,333

Dropout Rate

The general dropout rate is approximately 34.1% for all the stages; the percentage of those attending the final tests for all stages is 65.8%.

According to the statistics concerning adult education for academic year 1984/85 (see Appendices 2 and 3), the dropout rate should be as follows:

- *Literacy stage:* The average dropout rate in the literacy stage is 24.5%, of which 29% are men and 20% are women.

- *Intermediate stage:* The average dropout rate is 25.5%, of which 26% are men and 25.2% are women.

- *Secondary stage:* The average dropout rate is 25.5%, of which 24% are men and 27.3% are women.

According to the statistics of the Examinations Department of the Administration of Adult Education, the percentage of those having passed their exams for the first term of 1984/85 is as follows:

Table 3
Percentage of Success achieved in the Examination
for the First Term of 1984-1985

STAGE	MALES	FEMALES
Literacy	69%	80.1%
Intermediate	62%	75.3%
Secondary	19.9%	28.5%
The general secondary exam	38%	42.2%

New figures have been added to the statistics as a result of the first term tests of the academic year 1984/85, which counts 13,423 graduates and dropouts from literacy and adult education classes, of which 7,534 are male and 5,889 are female. New figures will also be added after the second term tests in September.

According to the 1980/81 statistics for all stages, only sixteen thousand students passed their exams and graduated, which was just before the literacy campaign. However, the literacy campaign brought greater awareness of the importance of literacy and adult education, which increased the number of students. By 1984 the figure nearly doubled to forty thousand students. (15)

The Permanent Committee for Information on Literacy in the Ministry of Education offered orientation programmes which proved to be vital.

Statistics on age groups have been very important in pointing out the critical situation of literacy, in addition to the statistics concerning the types of skills in the centres in 1984/85, which led to the following conclusion:

Centres for men (see Appendices 4 and 5)

- The highest rate of male enrolment falls in the category of 15 to 39 years old, i.e. the working age

- The largest group is between 20 and 30 years old

- Kuwaiti males account for 53% of enrolment

- The largest participant groups are from: the armed forces, the unemployed, guards and civil servants.

Centres for women

- The rate of female enrolment falls in the category of 15 to 39 years old.

- Within this age group the greatest percentage are between 15 and 19 years old, which is generally the marrying age for girls, thus preventing them from continuing their education in public schools. Therefore, they join adult centres for the intermediate and secondary stages.

- Kuwaiti females account for 65% of enrolment. (See Appendix 5)

- Housewives represent the main participant group enrolled with 95% of the total female students in all the stages, followed by a group of housemaids and servants.

Preparation of the Comprehensive Literacy Campaign

It was necessary to re-assess the efforts undertaken for literacy education in order to change the focus on illiteracy as an education problem concerning a limited sector of society to a global view that must encourage both individuals and organizations to participate effectively in facing the problem of illiteracy as one that affects the different groups of society and its development.

The Law issued for compulsory literacy education

On January 11, 1981 Law No. 4 was issued with twenty-three articles (see Appendix 6), followed by an Emirate decree on August 8, 1981 defining the compulsory literacy law and the groups that fall under this legal obligation. The law was ratified by a speech given by His Highness, the Ruling Prince, on August 24, 1981 in which he also gave the green light to exert maximum efforts in that direction. (16)

The Legal definition of illiteracy and the obligations for its eradication

Article 1 stipulates that "literacy is a national obligation", thus transferring it from a purely individual duty to a national one. Prior to the Article, responsibility for literacy depended on the efforts of the illiterate himself or just one sector in particular, i.e. the Ministry of Education.

This Article also stipulates the importance of employing the necessary resources in order to improve both the social and cultural level of illiterates, thereby upgrading his or her standard of living and benefitting society as well. This attitude is adapted to the cultural concept of functional literacy education.

Legal definition of an illiterate

The law defines the illiterate as "someone who has reached the age of fourteen and is not yet at the fourth grade of the primary stage in the level of writing, reading and counting, and is not registered in an elementary school".

Groups falling under the compulsory law

- Illiterate Kuwaities who exceed the compulsory age group according to Law No. 11 of 1965, i.e. those aged fourteen to forty years old.

- Kuwaiti females working in the government sector between the ages of fourteen and thirty-five.

Flexibility in absorbing all the illiterates

According to Article 2, all persons of fourteen years of age and above who do not fall in the above-mentioned categories may voluntarily join a literacy programme.

Gradual implementation of compulsory literacy

Compulsory literacy began to be implemented during the 1981/82 academic year for illiterates between the ages of fourteen and forty working in government establishments, public organizations and government-shared companies. Female illiterates between the ages of fourteen and thirty-five working in the government sector are required to participate in education.

In 1982/83 liability for literacy education encompassed all males meeting the conditions of the compulsory law, i.e. falling in the age group of fourteen to forty, whether employed or not. The implementation for females remained the same as in the previous year.

Levels of obligation in the implementation of the law

The law stipulates the various levels of responsibility towards literacy:

(a) Individual obligation

Article 3 in the law stipulates that every individual, including working women, is under obligation to register at the nearest centre for literacy, regularly attend classes and take the tests.

The aims of Articles 3 and 10 are to treat the considerable problems of literacy education as well as absenteeism from classes and year-end tests. The Articles also resolved the problem of gathering illiterates together by compelling them to register their names in centres.

(b) Obligation of organizations

The law obligates all official groups and organizations as well as private sector enterprises to participate in the planning, follow-up and implementation of compulsory literacy education.

The Planning Field

Higher Committee for Literacy Education

Certain ministries are obligated by law to co-operate with experts concerned with literacy education in both the public and private sectors to plan and organize a comprehensive literacy campaign at the national level.

In conformity with this principle a higher committee was formed under the chairmanship of the Minister of Education and composed of representatives of certain sectors to draw

up outlines of the campaign policy and to regulate prize-
giving and incentives for students. The following are representatives of certain sectors:

Ministry of Education
Ministry of Planning
Ministry of Social Affairs and Labour
Ministry of Information
Ministry of Interior Affairs
Ministry of Waqf and Islamic Affairs
Faculty of Education in the University of Kuwait
Five experts from the private sector
Director of the Administration of Adult Education
    and Literacy

Temporary committees for planning the campaign

The following committees are in charge of laying the
necessary groundwork for the implementation of the law:

Information Committee
Technical Committee
Statistics Committee
Health Committee

The plans are drawn up by temporary committees for the
permanent committees which implement them and follow them
up.

Permanent committees for the implementation of the
literacy law

The Higher Committee created four other permanent committees which convert the articles of the law into work programmes and implement a follow-up of the accredited plans
by the Higher Committee for Literacy Education. The committees are:

- Permanent Committee for Literacy Information in which
  the following have participated:

. Ministry of Information
. Ministry of Waqf
. Ministry of Social Affairs
. Association of Instructors

. Ministry of Education
. General Department for Vocational Education and
  Training

- Permanent Technical Committee from the University and
  Higher Education

- Legal and Financial Committee from the administrative,
  financial and legal departments in the Ministry of Education

- Supervisory Committee for the Legal Implementation of
  the Law from the Administration of Literacy and Adult
  Education.

*The General Obligation of Certified Illiterates with
Consideration to the Different Circumstances Facing them*

The law has also taken into consideration the circumstances of illiterates subject to compulsory literacy education
in the two following areas:

For certified illiterates

Health and social problems have been taken into consideration in exempting the ill or handicapped from regular education programmes. However, the exemption is withdrawn
once the cause has been cleared up. In case an illiterate
has difficulty in registering on time, a postponement may
be granted by ministerial decree. This is a form of flexibility to the law which takes into consideration the
various social and health problems of the illiterate individual.

For private enterprises and their employees

The Ministry of Education's law authorizes the opening of
classes on the working sites of enterprises when there
are more than twenty-five workers. This measure has been
inspired by the working problems which face this group of
learners.

The law has taken into consideration the co-ordination of
the learning hours with regard to the official working
hours to avoid any possible inconvenience. It also requires the enterprise owners to facilitate the enrolment
of illiterates in the literacy course.

*Incentives and Control in Order to Facilitate the
Implementation of the Law*

Incentives

Among the various incentives offered is the authorization
of learners who read and write but have not obtained a
literacy certificate to attend the annual exams in order
to define their academic standing. Those who have passed
the exams are exempt from obligatory attendance in a literacy class and may move on to the intermediate stage.
Those who have not passed the exam will be registered in
a literacy class according to their level.

The regulations have been set in order to determine the
academic level of the students who have obtained a literacy certificate from one of the primary stages, i.e. from
grade one to grade three, thus placing them in the appropriate class.

Transport granted to female students

The Ministry of Education provides female students with
transportation to their classes.

Financial and moral support

Article 14 of the law stipulates that financial rewards
are to be presented at a graduation ceremony to outstanding students in the presence of their friends, colleagues
and community, with press and television coverage for the
occasion. The rewards are meant to encourage those who
have excelled and to stimulate others to do likewise.

Special learning leaves for workers to attend exams

By law a special leave must be granted to working students
in order to attend exams without deducting time from their
annual leave. This reflects the right that has been granted to students of adult education to pursue their education in both the intermediate and secondary stages.

Introduction of complementary programmes of social and cultural activities as a form of incentive

The activities for both male and female learners through-

out all the education stages are supervised by the social and
cultural section and include the following:

- Annual contests for adults that will allow them to
  practice their education skills and acquire more knowledge. These contests could include the preparation of
  scientific, social and health research.

- An annual exhibition for the students' artistic works,
  handicrafts, wall newspapers, typed magazines, embroidery, etc. The exhibition is organized by the students
  themselves under the supervision of the social and
  cultural programme which will award prizes for the best
  works.

- An annual community health orientation programme for
  adults in co-ordination with the Ministry of Health,
  wherein medical doctors of various specializations
  would give lectures concerning health in all the centres and for all stages. Topics would be selected in
  order to broaden students' community health education,
  as well as to increase their awareness of environmental
  hazards and preventive methods.

- Celebrations for the various religious and national
  occasions with open invitations to the public, as well
  as a special prize-giving day for graduates of literacy
  classes.

- Publication of a magazine for adult education in five
  issues for the whole year, offering educational content
  as well as an opportunity for students to participate
  and thus demonstrate their skills and talents. As a
  form of encouragement, financial prizes are offered for
  the contests found in each magazine.

  The magazine aims at opening new horizons of culture
  and knowledge and also offers an opportunity for students to discover their talents and attract other students to join the centres, thereby creating a direct
  relationship with the community and spreading culture.

The Main Regulations Guaranteeing Implementation of the Law

Prohibition of employing any illiterate Kuwaiti

Article 16 prohibits the employment of an illiterate Kuwaiti in any kind of organization or public establishment unless he or she is enrolled in a literacy centre.

Preventing the promotion of any illiterate employee

Article 17 stipulates that no illiterate employee or worker may receive a promotion unless he or she obtains a literacy certificate. One the certificate is obtained he or she automatically receives the promotion that was blocked during his education period.

Financial penalties for violation of law

Penalties are imposed on all those who:

- have not registered at a literacy centre

- have exceeded the allowed period of absenteeism (25% of the academic year) without a valid excuse.

Compulsory rules for employers

As per Article 20 a financial penalty is imposed on any employer for infringement of the literacy law. The severity of the penalty depends on the number of workers who have transgressed the law, and this penalty may be doubled in case of repeated violations. The following are situations which inculpate the employer for the illiteracy of his workers:

(a) Employers disregarding the learning hours of their workers and dismissing them for that reason or reducing their salary if they continue to attend classes.

(b) Employers hindering education by making it difficult for the workers to enrol in a literacy class.

(c) Employers abstaining from reporting the names of workers employed to the Ministry of Education within the prescribed sixty-day period.

(d) Employers disregarding the promotion law, granting a promotion regardless of a literacy certificate.

Table 4

Number of Male and Female Learners
registered in Literacy Classes from the Beginning
of the Campaign in 1981/82 to 1984/85 (17)

Academic Year	Number of males	Number of females	Total
1981/82	6 998	5 048	12 046
1982/83	5 498	4 637	10 135
1983/84	5 469	4 556	10 025
1984/85	5 571	4 681	10 252
Total	23 536	18 922	42 458

Development of the Efforts Undertaken in Literacy and Adult Education

Quantitative development in numbers and sex

The strategy of literacy and adult education has increased quantitatively and qualitatively in the following manner:

The literacy education of certain groups of workers was limited because class books used were those assigned to children in the primary stage of public education. Later on, efforts were increased, with the institution of separate literacy education classes for males and females.

Progress in the duration and planning of education

Initially, the duration of literacy education lasted four academic years of eight months per year, five days per week (excluding Thursday and Friday) with two lessons per day, totalling ten lessons per week. Until the academic year 1965/66 this was the standard system for literacy education. Subsequent to the academic year 1965/66 the duration of the literacy course was reduced to two years of nine months per year and the number of lessons was increased to three per day, totalling fifteen per week. This revision in the duration of the course came as the result of intensive studies to reduce the students' learning period.

The distribution of weekly lessons was as follows:

- 9 reading and writing lessons

- 4 arithmetic lessons

- 2 Islamic education lessons.

Development of the textbooks and the method of instruction (literacy stage)

In order to adapt to the requirements of adults, course books have changed more than once. From the beginning of literacy education until 1959/60, children's books were employed; from 1960 through to 1965 a collection of books for literacy education was compiled for both men and women. The books for language, arithmetic and Islamic education were revised to adapt to the new two-year period of education and to the education requirements of students. Since 1966/67 the books have not changed.

The *Teacher's Manual* was published in order to help students assimilate more easily the syllabus and also help instructors in carrying out their tasks. This manual presents all the subjects in a suitable manner for students, for the whole syllabus is given by one instructor, the class teacher, during the whole literacy course.

By 1976/77 the system of one class teacher was revamped and the three subjects were then taught by three different specialized instructors who followed a specific technical guidance course in order to assure effective instruction.

Quantitative and qualitative development in offering post-literacy education (continuing education)

The literacy education programme developed into a continuing adult education programme which led to opening classes for adults at both the intermediate and secondary stages, with art and science sections at the secondary stage. Classes at the intermediate stage were underway in 1963/64 for men and in 1966/67 for women. Secondary stage classes started up in 1967/68 and a large number of male and female students enrolled.

Cultural community health programmes were introduced in 1975/76 by the Adult Education Planning Programmes in order to widen the scope of education. The programmes were implemented under the supervision of the specialized Technical Guidance Department of the Administration.

Progress in confronting literacy

Law No. 4 was issued in 1981 as a means of ending both illiteracy and cultural deprivation by stipulating compulsory attendance in a literacy class for illiterate men between the ages of fourteen and forty and illiterate women between the ages of fourteen and thirty-five. This law is the outcome of the comprehensive campaign against illiteracy begun in 1981/82.

A number of measures were taken in order to encourage illiterates and students in literacy classes by offering prizes and financial rewards to all those who passed their annual exams with good grades.

Development of supervision and expenditures for adult education programmes

The supervision was performed by the Administration of Social and Labour Affairs and the Education Department. It is to be handed over to the complete responsibility of the Ministry of Education.

4. POST-LITERACY STAGE AND CONTINUING EDUCATION

4.1 Expansion in the Efforts and Educational Programmes for Post-literacy Education

Form 1958 to 1981 the policy for literacy education developed from limited efforts for adult literacy to the possibility of continuing education at the intermediate stage. The next development was the continuation of adult education to the secondary stage in both the science and art sections and eventually advancement to a university education. This development was the result of both the students' desire to continue their education and the state's plan to develop human resources and thus open a new sphere for continuing education.

The first classes in the intermediate stage for males were opened in 1959/60. These included only the first grade of the intermediate stage. In 1963/64 the project was completed and the four grades of the intermediate stage were made available. This stage became accessible to female students in 1966/67.

The first secondary centre for men was opened in 1966/67 and for women in 1967/68. During that same year thirty-five literacy and adult education centres were made available, counting 17,039 male students and 80 female students. The large development that took place may be observed by comparing the numbers of centres and enrolments between 1957/58 and 1967/68. (18)

The development from literacy to post-literacy education in Kuwait has proved to be a positive and active step forward for continuing education, which encompasses a continuum from literacy to university education and post-graduate studies.

The Ministry of Education has offered every possible opportunity in order to fulfill Kuwait's major objective, which is to offer each individual the opportunity of acquiring education. It is important at this point to note the integral, par-

allel and differential aspects between public education and
adult education.

4.2   The Integral, Parallel and Differential Aspects between
      Literacy and Adult Education and Public Education, within
      the Framework of Continuing Education

Aspects of Integration

The aspects of integration between adult and public education (for the young) are as follows:

(a) The fulfillment of the general objectives of com-
    prehensive education

    Adult and public education are integrated within the
    objectives of comprehensive education, which include
    making education available to every individual in the
    country and offering an opportunity of continuing
    education according to the desires and qualifications
    of the students.

(b) Integration in providing necessary possibilities for
    adult education

    One of the main aspects of integration in this field
    is employing public day-school facilities for evening
    literacy and adult classes. These schools have the
    advantage of being conveniently located and available
    throughout most of the country, in addition to the
    educational equipment, furniture, lighting, labora-
    tories and utilities available which facilitate the
    education of adults.

    These schools are now known as centres, in order to
    distinguish them from formal schools and highlight
    their function as education facilities for adults.

    This integration has helped reduce the costs of adult
    education in addition to the time and effort saved in
    having ready-made buildings adequately equipped and
    conveniently located. Therefore adult centres are
    constructed (quite rapidly) only in areas where they
    are required.

(c) Integration in technical and human power

Teachers are chosen from public education schools to instruct adults in literacy and adult education centres according to the required specializations. The technical guides of different specializations and education levels are also selected from these schools so as to offer the necessary services to instructors. The whole process is supervised by the Administration for Adult Education and the specialized organizations. This saves employment costs; not including the general personnel, some 3,557 instructors are involved.

Aspects of Parallelism Between Public Education and Adult Education

(a) On the education level:

The education level is parallel at the three stages of adult education: literacy, intermediate and secondary. Students receiving a general secondary certificate from an adult centre are as qualified for a university education as public education school graduates. They can study in any faculty or institute according to their specializations and grades.

Between 1969 and 1985, 61,603 students - out of 303,918 students registered during that period - graduated from adult centres at the different educational stages.

The following table indicates the breakdown of graduates for each stage of adult education between 1969-1985:

Table 5

Classification of Graduates According to Sex
and Education Level between 1969-1985

Stage	Number of graduates (male and female)		Ratio of graduates to students registered
Literacy	37 675		28.9%
Intermediate	20 465		18%
Secondary	12 923		13.6%
Total	61 063	average %	20.1%

(b) The syllabus:

There is total parallelism with respect to syllabus
and books in both public education and adult education
(post-literacy education), as far as the intermediate
and secondary stages are concerned. At the literacy
stage the syllabus and books differ between the literacy programme and public education (primary stage),
however the skills that are taught are the same.

(c) Sequence in the vertical education scale:

The ascending sequence of education is parallel, with
the exception of kindergarten in the primary stage
where the primary, intermediate and secondary stages
in public education are analogous to the literacy,
intermediate and secondary stages in adult education.

The same parallelism is also found in the duration of
both the intermediate and secondary stages where each
stage is four academic years, whereas the literacy
stage is two years.

(d) Graduates:

Graduates of both public and adult education pro-

grammes are equally qualified, and those who have
completed their secondary education may join universities depending on their grades; both may also undertake post graduate studies if they wish. Graduates
also have equal chances of employment, of improving
their functional levels and of benefitting from the
various training programmes offered.

*Differential Aspects Between Adult, Literacy and Public
Education*

(a) Academic planning:

Academic planning for literacy programmes differs
from that for adult education, insofar as the latter
is concentrated in a limited number of hours in the
evening courses (two-and-a-half or three-and-a-half
hours). Limiting the number of hours for adults is a
means of allowing them to go back home after their
work in order to finish whatever they have to do at
home before going to their classes. The classes offered in public schools that are not available to
adult students are physical education, art and music
education, and home economics. Therefore during the
intermediate and secondary stages the number of
classes for a public school student is 30 to 32 per
week compared with 20 to 22 classes for an adult student. The same applies for the literacy stage, where
students are given 15 classes instead of the 30
classes of a primary stage pupil.

(b) Starting age:

The difference in the starting age between both forms
of education is that school pupils go to school at
the age of four in kindergarten and at the age of six
in form one primary stage, whereas students in adult
education start at the age of fourteen or above in
the literacy classes. They generally belong to the
following groups:

- Illiterates who never enrolled in the primary stage
  of a school and are above the admission age

- Students who have finished the literacy course and
  want to continue their education at the intermediate

and secondary stages

- Students who for one reason or another could not adjust to the formal school system and joined adult centres to continue their education, in certain cases while holding jobs

- Workers who were obliged to quit their education and never received any certificate to indicate their level of education before dropping out and joined an adult centre in order to acquire this certificate which may open doors for promotion in their work.

(See Figure 2 on structure of vertical and horizontal parallelism. p. 168)

Horizontal Parallelism

(a) Number of years:

The number of years for the intermediate and secondary stages of both public and adult education programmes are the same, i.e. four years for each stage. The difference exists between the four years of the primary stage of public education and the two years of the literacy programme.

(b) Adapting the curriculum in the development stage:

Since the principle of parallelism in the development of the personality and education in both adult and public education is to reach an integration of the physical, intellectual, spiritual and moral personality, the difference between an adult student and a school pupil cannot be ignored. Therefore the curriculum, which is basically geared to school students, needs to be revised for adults. This was the case for the literacy stage in order to adapt to the experience, age and life style of adults, while retaining the same level of education as in public education.

(c) Characteristics of adult education:

The aspects of differences specific to adult education programmes provided by the different systems in view

168

Receiving the genl secondary certificate qualifying learners for any job	Continuing education in the university according to the specific avg.	Enrolment in applied institutes for continuing education	Qualification for specific government training programmes and various seminars

Graduates at the end of the secondary stage

Extent of vertical parallelism

Kindergarten — Primary stage — Inter. stage — Second. stage — Second. stage — Intermediate stage — Literacy stage

4 yrs.

4 yrs.

4 years

4 years

4 years

2 years

Kindergarten found in traditional school systems

No kindergarten for adults

⟵ Horizontal parallelism

Public Education	Specific Education
Public schools — Private schools	Literacy & Adult Education
Incipience in public schools	1 - Children 4 yrs. old for kindergarten 2 - 6-14 yrs. old during primary stage, etc.	1 - Male & female adults above 14 years old 2 - Students transferring from public educ. schools 3 - Employees who had to end their educ.	Incipience of literacy and adult education

Figure 2: Vertical and Horizontal Parallelism between Formal and Literacy Education

of facilitating and assisting adult students throughout their education are numerous.

(d) During the period of learning:

The literacy and adult education courses are given in
the evening and for a limited period of time compared
with public education, allowing students to assume
their professional, vocational and social duties
while continuing their education, which is a considerable advantage.

(e) Admission age:

The admission age for adults is fourteen years old
and above with no restriction, which again is another
advantage. Except in certain cases students under
fourteen years of age may not enrol according to the
compulsory education law.

(f) Examination system:

Unlike public education in which students have to sit
for weekly tests and monthly exams as well as end-of-
term exams, adults at all stages sit for one end-of-
year exam, which is also another advantage. This is
also a way of facilitating their education in view of
their circumstances, which may otherwise prevent them
from regularly attending tests and exams. Therefore
an end-of-year exam is given, covering subjects
studied throughout the year (during the secondary
stage). In the public education schools, the pupils
will be examined on half the syllabus each term, but
for both systems of education, the end-of-year exam
is the same, covering the entire syllabus. During the
secondary stage, students from both systems of education sit for their exams together; during the literacy and intermediate stages, students take their
exams in the evenings in the centres for adult education.

4.3   The Method of Dealing with Students

Instructors deal with adults on a different level than
with younger pupils for the following reasons:

- In view of the experience, age and social position of adult students, who are sometimes older than their instructors, a special approach based on adult psychology is adopted by the instructors.

- Since adults at both the intermediate and secondary stages, and a part of the literacy stage, enrol voluntarily in adult education programmes, a wrong approach or misunderstanding on the part of the instructor may provoke students to abandon the course.

- Adults need encouragement to get over the inhibitions and hesitations which may occur when resuming their education at an advanced age.

4.4 Selection of Instructors and their Training

A number of criteria are considered in selecting the instructors, who are offered technical guidance according to the subject they teach in order to hone their professional performance. The selection criteria are:

- The psychological aptitude of the instructor for adults.

- The professional standard of the instructor in the public education school system.

- The benefit his or her subject of specialization will bring to the students.

- A minimum period of experience of not less than three years.

- A professional grade not less than good and preferably higher.

As a form of incentive an instructor is appointed on the basis of a yearly contract, which is renewable in case of good performance and cancelled if it is the contrary.

4.5 Motivational Devices

A set of measures and arrangements have been adopted in

order to facilitate post-literacy stage attendance and learning. The most important are the following:

Class Repeating

Students are not limited to a number of years before being expelled from a class since the age barrier is ignored and the homogeneity of the class is not affected.

This again is another advantage to this form of education since the aim is to encourage adults to pursue their education and attempt to obtain a certificate, provided they respect the attendance regulations.

Special Facilities for Adults

Both male and female students who work are granted special leaves for their education which permits them to attend end-of-year exams and which are not deductible from their other leaves.

Learners in the literacy stage in particular are allowed to repeat the tests in the second round if they failed in the first one. This is to give them more than one chance to continue their education and pass their literacy exams.

Special Community Cultural Programmes

A special Technical Guidance Department prepares community cultural programmes for adults concerning culture, sociology and health. These programmes are implemented by social experts.

5.   STRATEGIES OF POST-LITERACY EDUCATION AS PART OF CONTINUING
     EDUCATION

The post-literacy education strategies in Kuwait are as
numerous as adult circumstances. The strategies conform to
opening new doors of education for adults to guarantee the con-
tinuance of their acquired educational skills and to prevent a
relapse into illiteracy. It also aims at allowing students to
use their skills and pursue self-education.

5.1   Flexible Alternative Strategies in Post-literacy and
      Continuing Education

Alternative approaches have been established in adult
education in order to offer different learning opportunities to
the target population. The alternatives are the following:

(1) *Religious Evening Classes* (Institute):

    Institutes have been opened for adult students who
    have completed the intermediate stage of both adult
    centres and public schools and wish to specialize in
    Islamic studies. The duration of education in these
    institutes is four academic years, in which a special-
    ized Islamic programme is studied. Kuwait has five
    specialized institutes of which four are for men and
    one for women: the four male institutes are Kortoba,
    Al Hassan Al Basry, Ibn Tufail and Al Fahayhal Centre;
    the female institute is Al Adiliya. The centres are
    located in different areas of Kuwait and are very pop-
    ular, thus many more are expected to be opened accord-
    ing to demand in various other areas. Specialized in-
    structors teach in the centres under the supervision
    of specialized technical guides in Islamic studies.
    The administration for religious institutes organizes
    the supervision as part of specific administration in
    charge of supervising the religious education in day
    schools.

(2) *Parallel Education:*

This form of education has been established in order to absorb students who failed to continue the intermediate education in public schools for certain reasons. This system offers educational programmes and training for students to learn skills for technical functions such as electricity, construction, concrete, tanning, etc. which are needed by the country.

An evening centre for parallel education was opened to absorb adults who wish to join. Specialized instructors of various programmes teach and train the students both in the basic education programme and in workshops. Graduates receive a certificate enabling them to join the labour force in their field of specialization and find work immediately. Employers offer them advantages and encouragement since the demand is high.

(3) *Two Night Centres for Improving Handwriting (Calligraphy):*

Ten years ago the administration for adult education opened two centres for improving Arabic calligraphy. A centre for men was opened in the Kadsiya region and another for women in the Talitla centre of the Naqra region. Students may join the centres once they have received the intermediate certificate or any superior certificate and wish to study the art of Arabic calligraphy.

Initially these centres were opened for the training of instructors in public education schools in calligraphic skills so as to teach them to the students. It was later opened to the public.

The duration of the course is two years, after which students sit for an examination and receive a certificate known as a "certificate of improved calligraphy", which qualifies them to work for a newspaper or magazine or participate in calligraphy exhibitions. For the past eight years students have participated in the annual calligraphy painting exhibition organized by the Administration for Literacy and Adult Education.

(4) *Home Instruction for Students in the Secondary Stage:*

The Ministry offered the alternative of home instruction for adults who cannot regularly attend classes
in the centres for reasons linked with work or any
other reasons. This form of alternative education is
for students who wish to continue their education
during the secondary stage; they register their names
at the Ministry, together with a certificate for the
stages they have completed in secondary education.
This enables them to sit for end-of-year exams. Registration may be made each year up to the end of
December.

In this way the Administration offers a form of assistance and facility to this group of students by
allowing them to attend all the classes they wish,
especially science, mathematics and language (English
and French) without having to register in the centres.

5.2   Multipurpose Use of Academic Books as a Major Educational
       Policy

As already indicated, the integrative or parallel aspects
of the Adult Education and Public Formal School are reflected
in the systematic and multipurpose use made of the text books.

Literacy Stage

The intensity by the adult literacy stage calls for a
corresponding curriculum plan.

(1) The main differences between the syllabus and books
    of literacy education and public education can be
    summarized as follows:

    - Adult books have been specially adapted to their
      mentality and experiences, while including the same
      educational skills as those of the primary stage of
      public education.

    - There are fewer books for adults than for school
      students since the adult education programme is
      abridged.

- Adult reading and grammar books are divided into two parts during the second year. One part is for men and the other for women since the material in the books concerns the respective interests of each sex.

- Adult books include certain exercises for learning reading and writing skills.

- Cultural subjects are included in adult books in order to satisfy their needs and to offer them a wider range of education without having to specialize in a particular subject as part of the general cultural education programme. Additional cultural books for adults are part of the plan. (19)

(2) The following section presents the specification and content of books of the literacy stage:

Reading Books for First Form Literacy Stage:

Part 1:

This book is intended to teach male and female learners the basic elements of reading and writing with the necessary exercises in thirty-five lessons. Each lesson includes a sentence from the following topics:

Successful learner
Fishing
Hazards of speed
A glimpse of an Arab city
Labour is an honour
Honesty in work
A girl from Kuwait
General advice
Traffic regulations
A glimpse of a Kuwaiti city and island
An exercise in reading and writing the sentence.

This book contains 168 pages with reading and writing exercises. An *Instructor's Manual* has been compiled so as to facilitate the teacher's task during this stage.

Part 2:

This book includes 130 pages and is separate from
Part 1. Illustrations are inserted as a method of explanation, and language skills are taught in 39 lessons. Class instructors are also provided with a
manual.

By the time a student has come to the end of this
book, he or she should be able to write what is represented in the illustrations, form sentences and
put words in the proper order, which is the equivalent level of forms 1 and 2 of primary public education schools. Learners are given a special exercise
book with Part II to work in under the supervision
of the instructor.

Arithmetic Book for Form One Literacy Stage

A 160-page book is given to both male and female students with the latest methods of arithmetic for
adults. This book is prepared in consideration of the
intellectual and vocabulary levels of the learners in
solving the problems in the book. Each chapter includes notes and figures in order to assist the instructor.(20)

*Instruction of Islamic Education for First Form
Literacy Stage*

This educational subject has no printed books since
first year literacy students are not qualified to
read the verses of the Koran. Technical guidance is
therefore offered to instructors in order to instruct
them on the method of teaching religious texts to
students.

Books for Second Form Literacy Stage

- Reading and comprehension book for men:

This 293-page volume has been specially compiled
for men, with illustrations and linguistic exercises. The book is equivalent in its education
matter to third- and fourth-form primary public
education.

Instruction in language skills should be as follows:

The presentation of the topics must be attractive to learners

The writing must be legible with a proper sentence after each exercise in reading, writing and grammar. The topics may be divided as follows: Islamic, national, educational, social, historical and geographical, scientific, health, international and modern, national and local, concerning Kuwait and the Arab world.

An *Instructor's Manual* has been prepared to help instructors.

- Reading and comprehension book for women:

A separate 307-page book has been specially written for women. The same psychological and intellectual considerations have been included with certain variations in the skills which fulfill her needs as woman and mother.

The subjects in the book may be divided into the same categories as the book for men, with the following additions:

Child health
Child education
Family care, entitled "The Happy Home"
Educational topics entitled "Letter From a Mother to Her Son".

The reading books include a variety of cultural topics adapted to adult needs in a more generalized method than books for primary public education.

Arithmetic Books for Second Form Literacy Stage

The arithmetic book is for both men and women with consideration of the following points:

- Learners must fully understand what is being taught to them so that they can solve problems and analyse the reasons.

- The material being taught has to be equivalent to third and fourth grades of the public primary stage.

- The examples and solutions in the book have to fit the learner's reality and environment. The examples must also be appropriate to his level and the course syllabus.

Arithmetic skills are based on the four fundamentals of addition, subtraction, division and multiplication - including fractions. Again teachers are provided with a manual.(21)

Book on Islamic Education for Second Form Literacy Stage

One volume has been prepared for this subject since the language skills at this level are more advanced and learners may take this book home and study.

This book is divided into four parts and contains 85 pages.

Part I   - The Holy Koran
Part II   - Instruction of the doctrine
Part III - Instruction of the rituals
Part IV   - Teachings of the Prophet's tradition and other Islamic subjects.

Intermediate and Secondary Stages

The syllabus and books are the same for the two stages in public education schools and the adult centres. The following subjects are taught during the intermediate stage:

Arabic language, Islamic education, English language, mathematics, sciences and social studies.

During the secondary stage the subjects are as follows:

Islamic education, Arabic, French, mathematics, science and social studies.

There is no discrimination between sexes for the books are the same for both sexes. The subjects are taught with the equipment and material available in the day schools, including the laboratories.

The syllabus and method of teaching depend on the adult education policy.

5.3   Learning Strategies Using Magazines and Wall Newspapers

The administration for Literacy and Adult Education issued a magazine fifteen years ago. Until 1985 seventy issues of ten thousand copies each were distributed to male and female students in post-literacy courses.

The magazine's main thrust is to widen the field of writing and develop the creative potentials of students, in addition to providing general knowledge and information.

It is prepared with the cultural guidance of the Administration and has sixteen pages including covers. The back cover is composed of a photograph with a short text and the front cover has a photograph of an important site in the Arab and Islamic world. A special calligrapher writes the texts of the magazine in large letters to facilitate reading. The magazine is divided into the following parts, each part being limited to one page:

Introduction

A collection of verses from the Koran written in beautiful calligraphy suitable to and reflecting the beauty of the Koran.

Preface to the Issue

The preface is written by the Chairman of the Administration to the students and the centre's employees to stimulate their desire to carry on their activities in continuing educational programmes.

Feature on a Personality

Every issue presents an Arab, Islamic or international personality who has contributed to humanity or knowledge.

History Section

This part aims at offering an analysis of a period of history to students in order to inform them of historical events and their impact on the present.

Promotion of Islam

This page is dedicated to reply to all the detractors of Islam and its civilization in an objective and scientifically analytical method, to reinforce the sense of pride and belonging among students, as well as giving them the right information to enable them to reply to any criticism.

Knowledge and Life

Stories related on this page involve scientific discoveries which have enriched humanity.

Poetry

A page is dedicated to an Arab classical poem which is generally of religious or patriotic inspiration.

Family Corner

This page is generally addressed to housewives concerning family matters, as well as the woman's role in the making of a happy family, the education of children, etc.

Health Corner

The use of medicine, causes of illness and psychological health are all part of this page.

Short Story

A selection of Arabic short stories fill this page, usually including a wise and humourous aspect.

Proverbs and Maxims

Contest in Each Issue

Each issue of the magazine includes a contest with six questions concerning Arab and Islamic culture first and modern culture second. The questions are formulated with blanks for the students to fill in, and, at the end of the page, there is a small coupon for the student to write his or her name. The coupon is received by the Community Cultural Advisor who in turn gives it to the ad-

ministration. The coupon may also be sent by ordinary
mail. Once the answers have been sorted out, the ten best
answers receive a cash prize.

Laugh with Us

This page is dedicated to humourous writings by students.

A election of Writings by Students

This section of the magazine is composed of students'
writing. These pieces are signed, thus offering further
incentive.

Back-over Page

This page includes a photographic illustration of an Arab,
Islamic or Gulf country with a short historical text.

Magazines for Students in the Centres

The centre magazines are supervised and distributed by
the students. They distribute their magazines to other
centres during religious or national occasions. The magazines have different titles and chapters according to the
occasion they usually celebrate, such as the Prophet's
ascension to heaven, the Isra Wal Mi'rag, the Prophet's
birthday, Kuwait's national day, family day, etc.

Separate chapters include the activities and give a general idea of each respective centre with a brief descrip-
tion of the town or village in which that centre is located. The magazines also include poetry, short stories,
scientific research and humour.

During the annual adult exhibition, all the magazines are
displayed. A magazine usually numbers fifteen pages and
fifty copies are issued per year. Thus students find the
opportunity to express their educational skills and ideas
in creative self-instruction while developing their capa-
bilities.

Wall Newspapers

Wall newspapers provide an opportunity to develop adult
talents, which is part of the education policy. With the

co-operation groups, students prepare the illustrated wall newspapers. They organize their material in columns, written and illustrated, and thus create texts with adapted illustrations which are shown during the annual adult exhibition as well.

Instructors and cultural advisors often provide guidance to the students in preparing the wall newspapers both in writing and planning. This form of guidance is intended to encourage students to use their skills and develop them through the different methods of education.

5.4   Adult Education Programmes and Facilities for Post-literacy and Continuing Education and Training

Public Libraries

Libraries managed by the National Committee of Culture, Arts and Literature and affiliated with the Ministry of Education are found in different parts of Kuwait. All the different branches of science, ideas and knowledge are found in these libraries, which are open mornings and evenings.

The libraries have a system of book circulation and are equipped with lounges and study rooms. Lectures and de-bates are sometimes held in the study rooms, which are open to the public. Libraries are a source of continuing education for post-literacy students.

Centre for Community Services and Permanent Education of the Kuwait University

This centre aims at developing the scientific, artistic and cultural potential of its members, regardless of edu-cational background, age or qualifications. Instructors specialized in languages, accounting, arts, music, etc. teach in this night centre, which has received a positive response from adults in different sections of post-liter-acy education.

Labour Cultural Centre

This centre was opened for the literacy education of workers and offers post-literacy courses as well. It was one of the first literacy centres to be opened when the state began to contribute to literacy education. Cultural and entertainment films are shown in a special projection room in the centre, and members of the centre have access to a library, at times open to outsiders.

Studies are available to all adults during the follow-up period in the night centres for vocational training.

Continuing Education Centres Run by Other Associations

A number of institutions and associations are providing opportunities for further learning together with their specific activities.

Fourteen centres for learning the Koran are affiliated with the Ministry of Waqf and Islamic Affairs.

Center for Community Services affiliated with the State Service for Vocational Education and Training.

Association for Public Welfare

The Association is concerned with professional, vocational and social affairs in the community for which it organizes cultural, entertainment and training programmes. Its programmes constitute an opening to education and other associations are in contact with it, such as:

- Association of Kuwaiti Instructors

  This association helps to reinforce students during the holidays after each academic year by opening special classes for them. This association has a library and offers a number of cultural and educational activities to children and adults. Cultural, scientific and social debates are also held for the benefit of post-literacy students.

- Women's Association for Social Culture

  These centres handle sports and cultural activities and spread these activities throughout the country. The centres are supervised by the Ministry of Social and Labour Affairs.

The various activities attract young people who join the centres and attend the annual working camps that are organized. In the camps they learn about the environment and become involved in tree-planting projects and other services.

Such activities, in addition to the discussions and reading which take place, open new vistas of education.

Youth centres and sports clubs

These centres provide sports and cultural activities throughout the country. They are supervised by the Ministry of Social Affairs and Labour. Young people join the centres to participate in sports and cultural activities, and youth work camps are held annually in which they acquire environmental information and perform services such as planting trees, etc.

These activities open indirect educational channels through the discussions and reading as well as provide opportunities for physical education.

5.5   Co-operative Learning Programmes for Adults

Health Education Programme

The aims of the programmes are the following:

- The health and community culture of students at all the educational stages

- To support the efforts which have been undertaken to raise the standard of community health through the male and female students who can point out the centre's role

- First aid for home accidents

- To develop student health research projects concerning environmental problems.

Each year, with the co-operation of the Ministry of Health, the Department of Health Orientation and the adult education centres, the programmes are prepared and implemented between December and the end of February.

The subjects are selected as a result of a field survey of environmental health undertaken by the Department of Health Orientation of the Ministry of Health. The tabulation, with the name of the centre and medical doctors who have contributed to the programme, is drawn up once the subject has been defined.

The following are the departments which participated in presenting the lectures: Department of Community Health Orientation, Department of Health Units (external clinics), Department for Child and Maternity Health, School Health, First Aid and the Department of Preventive Health.

The subjects are divided into two parts, one for men and one for women, in addition to certain subjects for both sexes. The main subjects for men are:

Detriment of smoking
Nutrition
The concept of infection, disease and diabetes

5.6   Preparation of Adult Information Programmes in Cooperation with the Ministry of Information

In cooperation with the Ministry of Information and in particular with the Ministry's Literacy Information Committee, an Adult Information project was started in 1981-82 with the declared aim of raising consciousness about the importance of literacy and adult education.

An information plan in the form of a diagram has been prepared on the basis of consultation within the Ministry and the Committee. (see Appendix No. 6)

Some of the programmes:

TV programme on basic skills

This is an information programme within the framework of Post Literacy and Adult Education. It has been transmitted on a monthly basis for the last years and is 30 minutes in length.

Preparation of the Information Television Programmes

Sixteen promotional series on literacy and adult education have been prepared with the co-operation of the Permanent Committee for Information on Literacy and with the Al Nawras company for Artistic Productions. The series are short sketches of two to four minutes and are occasionally shown on television. The programmes have been televised in Kuwait with the co-operation of the Ministry of Information and Television.

Preparation of Short Films for Literacy Training

Five short promotional films to stimulate illiterates for literacy education were produced with the co-operation of the Ministry of Information and the Department of Cinema. Seventy copies of the films were made and distributed to the fourteen cinema theatres in Kuwait to be shown between regular shows.

Production of Radio Drama Serials

The Permanent Committee for Information on Literacy with the co-operation of the Ministry of Information's Radio Department produced a radio series called "Knowledge is Light". This radio programme aims at informing adults of the importance of adult education. Other radio programmes also support this orientation of literacy and adult education.

Orientation Programmes with the Co-operation of the Ministry of Waqf and Islamic Affairs

An annual orientation programme is prepared with the Ministry of Waqf and Islamic Affairs which involves Mosque preachers discussing the importance of adult education, especially for women. The Ministry has also distributed publications through the Committee for Literacy in all the populated areas.

Co-operation with the Local Press

A general awareness programme on the importance of literacy and adult education has been created in the local press in co-operation with the Permanent Committee for Literacy Information and the Public Rations Department of the Ministry of Education. The contribution of the press is as follows:

- Write press reports with students in the centres

- Write press reports with the centre supervisors and advisors responsible for the activities

- Make a coverage of the annual prize-giving day.

All these efforts aim at stimulating the participation and co-operation of each possible organization, establishment or department in supporting and reinforcing all the efforts undertaken in literacy and adult education, as well as informing the public of all the achievements and facilities offered to adult education.

Preparation of Information Pamphlets and Publications

The preparations involve:

- The preparation of information pamphlets with the co-operation of the Information Committee, the Administration of Printing Matters and the Administration for Adult Education

- The preparation of illustrated posters for illiterates

- The preparation of information press folders.

Preparation of Slides for Television

In order to diversify the methods of publicity for literacy and adult education, a collection of coloured slides showing the students and the centres was prepared in co-operation with the Administration of Education. The slides are projected in cinemas and on television as a means of spreading the orientation scope.

Organization of Celebrations and Invitations to Citizens

Each year between the 3rd and 30th of January a celebration is organized to point out the importance of adult education and its role in developing human resources. Graduates from literacy classes and regular attending students are honoured on that day and the public is invited to participate in the prize-giving ceremony. (22)

Information Co-operation With the Ministry of Interior Affairs

The Ministry of Interior Affairs has dedicated a section of its monthly magazine, *Interior Affairs*, to literacy and adult education. The Permanent Committee for Literacy has also contributed.

A campaign Logo

Among the major steps adopted from the start was the design of a logo for the literacy campaign, which was printed on certificates for students, various publications and particularly on all the shopping bags of the Association of Co-operatives in each region. The design of the logo represents the transition period between past and present as fulfilled by education in Kuwait. This initiative was undertaken as one of the forms of general promotion for adult education.

5.7   Other Supporting Programmes and Activities

Exhibition for Adult Learners

For the past ten years an annual exhibition has been organized for all adult intellectual and artistic activities, which often include handicrafts such as embroidery, etc. This exhibition is viewed as a major incentive for students to practice their acquired educational skills in a creative form, which is all part of an indirect method of education within the framework of continuing education.

This exhibition takes place at the end of the academic year, which is the end of April, and includes the following activities:

- Printed magazines prepared by students throughout the year

- Wall newspapers prepared by students throughout the year

- Calligraphy paintings

- Photography

- Plastic arts and environmental projects

- Embroidery from female centres

- Other projects.

During the annual celebration the centres compete, as do individual learners, for first place; cups and shields are awarded as prizes. Citizen attendance is quite high at the exhibit, which receives television and press coverage. The higher officials of the Ministry of Education, and in most cases the Undersecretary of the Ministry, in person, inaugurate the exhibition as a form of encouragement to the learners.

Each centre has a designated section which is organized by that centre's students. They are responsible for the posters and other written material exhibited and they greet the public and explain their work.

Different Research

The preparation of scientific, literary, social, economic, traditional Islamic and health research is a method of post-literacy education. Students prepare papers for annual contests based on research topics selected by various instructors who define the subject and provide students with titles of necessary reference material. The research outline provided to the learner includes the following guidelines:

- The research must include every aspect of the subject.

- Support the research with the documentation and references used as well as any necessary statistics and illustrations.

- The paper cannot be less than nine pages and not more than twelve pages.

- The student must be prepared to discuss his research paper once it has been prepared.

Evaluation grades are defined as follows:

- Maximum grade is 100

- Passing grade is 60

Grades on research papers are given as follows:

- Completeness of subject is worth 40 points

- Good composition and arrangement is worth 20

- Use of references and statistics is worth 20

- Discussion is worth 20

Financial prizes are offered, as well as certificates of appreciation, for the best research papers, which are bound and indexed by the name of the student. The Administration is planning to start publishing the research papers in the adult education magazines as a form of encouragement to the students.(23)

6. CONCLUSION

In addition to all that has been said concerning the comprehensive development in post-literacy and continuing education
strategies, the following may be pointed out:

The concept of continuing education in Kuwait springs
from its firm conviction in the teachings of Islam, which stress
the quest for knowledge, the importance of a religious education
and a familiarity with world affairs, thus fulfilling the meaning of existence. The age factor should never stand in the way
of knowledge: "Seek knowledge from birth until death" says the
Koran. Nor is it limited to place, "Seek knowledge, be it in
China", nor does a discrimination of sexes prevent that quest,
"The quest for knowledge is a Divine ordinance for every Muslim
man and women".

In an age of scientific explosion, Kuwait believes in
each individual's right and responsibility to live in his time
with an open mind and an awareness of both personal and social
duties. It also believes that adults are an important and vital
human resource since they are parents who will educate and
train the forthcoming generations in addition to being an important source for production.

In Kuwait, the relation between literacy and adult education as part of continuing education and the development programmes is a very close one. Therefore the first step was reading literacy for adults, which developed into legislated compulsory education. This later developed into the possibility for
adults to continue their post-literacy education throughout the
intermediate and secondary stages and eventually to go as far
as university studies.

Statistics on the number of graduates of adult education
centres have already been mentioned in this study.

Another step forward undertaken by the state, which has

always been concerned with this problem, is the Compulsory Education Law No. 11 (1965), stipulating the obligatory education of children from the age of six through to fourteen. This law was implemented in 1966/67. In the same spirit, adult education centres were opened in every area with all the necessary human and material resources.

The culmination of all these efforts resulted in Law No. 4, which imposed literacy education in January 1981. The law was actually implemented during the academic year 1981/82 as part of the comprehensive campaign (see Appendix No. 7).

Literacy and adult education began to develop with the implementation of cultural programmes falling under the concept of cultural literacy in agreement with the general Arab strategy for literacy. It has also paved the way for self-instruction and continuing education so as to prevent a relapse into illiteracy.

Among the major developments was the spreading of efforts previously undertaken by the Ministry of Education alone among other departments and organizations for planning, following up and implementing the programmes, with the technical and organizational support of the Ministry of Education. A considerable decrease in the rate of illiteracy has been achieved as a result of these efforts, which was determined by the census of the total ten-year-old-and-over age group. The tables figuring in this study indicate the thousands of adult graduates from the various stages who have joined universities or institutes.

However, certain problems remain to be solved and still hinder the objectives of literacy and adult education. We believe this is to be expected; there is no doubt that these problems remain the same everywhere. However, Kuwait has made great strides and still continues to do so in the field of literacy and adult education.

One of Kuwait's main objectives is the quest for new forms of educational and cultural programmes to adapt to the needs of the society and the aims of the development plans. In this respect, the future goals set for adult education are the following:

(a) The total eradication of illiteracy in Kuwait

(b) Continuation of adult education (post-literacy education) towards self-instruction and continuing education

(c) The opening of new fields of employment for the educational skills of adults in vocational training which accompany educational programmes adapted to both men and women in their different interests

(d) The development of the programme, syllabus and curriculum for adult education to adapt to students' lifestyles while retaining the content and educational level of public education schools

(e) The publication of a number of supplementary books for adults concerning different aspects of modern life and traditions as a means of inculcating them within the framework of an objective approach to life.

In the field of regional and international co-operation, Kuwait untiringly continues to exert the maximum efforts to link the concept of adult education to continuing education with the help of all the relevant organizations both regionally and internationally. Among these organizations are the Arab Organization for Cultural and Scientific Education, the Arab Organization for Literacy Education and UNESCO.

APPENDIX 1

Statistics Based on the Census of the Number of Kuwaiti
Illiterates 10-Years-Old and Above

Years of the general count	Sex	Kuwaities 10-years-old and above	Illiterates 10-years-old and above	%
57	males	38 461	34 420	89.5
	females	35 287	32 363	91.7
	total	73 748	66 783	90.5
Total population		107 246	66 783	62.3
65	males	70 859	56 977	80.4
	females	67 169	59 832	89
	total	138 028	116 809	84.6
Total population		220 059	116 809	53
70	males	110 846	67 183	60.6
	females	108 246	81 660	75.4
	total	219 092	148 843	67.9
Total population		347 396	148 843	42.8
75	males	149 654	76 167	50.8
	females	150 120	101 387	67.5
	total	299 774	177 554	59.2
Total population		472 088	177 554	
80	males	178 796	72 914	40.7
	females	185 740	111 975	60.2
	total	364 536	184 889	50.7
Total population		565 613	184 889	32.6

APPENDIX 2

Statistics on Male Dropouts from Literacy and Adult Education Centres
at the End of April During Academic Year 1984/1985

Centre for Men

	Literacy stage			Intermediate stage					Secondary stage							Total stages
	1st lit.	2nd lit.	Total of stage	1st int.	2nd int.	3rd int.	4th int.	Total of stage	1st sec.	2nd sec.	3rd sec. Arts	3rd sec. Sci.	4th sec. Arts	4th sec. Sci.	Total of stage	
Reg. end Oct.	3576	2065	5641	2717	1912	1813	2190	8632	5746	2909	1402	203	1550	464	12284	26557
Reg. end Apr. drop-outs	2505	1863	4368	1645	1543	1535	2086	6809	3871	2423	1363	190	1681	443	9971	21148
Total drop-outs	1071	202	1273	1072	369	278	104	1823	1875	486	39	13	--	21	2434	5530
% of drop-outs	42%	10%	29%	65%	23%	18%	4%	26%	48%	20%	2%	6%	--	4%	24%	26%

Abbreviations: lit. = literacy
int. = intermediate
sec. = secondary
Sci. = Science
Reg. = Registered

APPENDIX 3

Statistics on Female Dropouts from Literacy and Adult Education Centres at the End of April During Academic Year 1984/85

Centre for Women

	Literacy stage			Intermediate stage					Secondary stage							Total stages
	1st lit.	2nd lit.	Total of stage	1st int.	2nd int.	3rd int.	4th int.	Total of stage	1st sec.	2nd sec.	3rd sec.	3rd sec.	4th sec.	4th sec.	Total of stage	
Reg. end Oct.	2755	1920	4675	1834	1221	863	845	4763	1530	969	506	132	644	220	4001	13 439
Reg. end Apr.	2244	1506	3750	1227	950	673	712	3562	866	701	438	112	601	190	2908	10 220
Total drop-outs	511	414	925	607	271	190	133	1201	664	268	68	20	43	30	1093	3 219
% of drop-outs	18.5	21.5	20.0	33.0	22.2	22.0	15.7	25.2	43.4	27.7	13.4	15.1	6.7	13.6	27.3	24.0

Abbreviations: lit. = literacy   Sci. = Science
                int. = intermediate   Reg. = Registered
                sec. = secondary

APPENDIX 4

Breakdown of Female Students by Age Group
at the End of April During Academic Year 1984/1985

Centres for Women

Age / Stage	Less than 14		15-19		20-24		25-29		30-34		35-39		40-44		45 - above		Total		GRAND TOTAL
	K	NK	K	NK	K	NK	K	NK	K	NK	K	NK	K	NK	K	NK	K	NK	
Literacy	21	94	397	738	250	354	229	238	289	116	307	74	251	57	291	44	2035	1715	3750
Intermediate	2	10	621	533	613	282	342	146	301	84	252	35	206	18	107	10	2444	1118	3562
Secondary	--	--	661	313	884	261	470	102	93	32	53	14	7	11	5	2	2173	735	2908
Total	23	104	1679	1584	1747	897	1041	486	683	232	612	123	464	86	403	56	6652	3568	10220

Percentage of Kuwaities: 65%

APPENDIX 5

Breakdown of Male Students by Age Group at the End of April During Academic Year 1984/1985

Centres for Men

Age \ Stage	Less than 14		15-19		20-24		25-29		30-34		35-39		40-44		45-above		Total		GRAND TOTAL
	K	NK	K	NK	K	NK	K	NK	K	NK	K	NK	K	NK	K	NK	K	NK	
Literacy	1	124	171	369	215	367	285	675	330	414	459	264	440	129	94	31	1995	2373	4368
Inter-mediate	-	-	796	752	751	739	643	957	440	701	306	338	139	121	92	34	3167	3642	6809
Second-ary	-	-	1180	883	2755	1295	1428	885	606	479	167	200	41	47	8	15	6167	3804	9971
Total	1	124	2147	2004	3721	2401	2356	2517	1376	1594	932	802	620	297	194	80	11329	9819	21148

Percentage of Kuwaities: 53%

APPENDIX 6

Breakdown of Illiterates
by Age - 1980

	Illiterate men			Illiterate women			GRAND
Age	Illt.	R&W	Total	Illt.	R&W	Total	TOTAL
10-14	2927	10800	13727	8706	9880	18586	32 313
15-19	2484	1239	3723	8711	1348	10059	13 782
20-24	2808	2041	4849	10140	1439	11579	16 428
25-29	2891	2332	5223	11038	1519	12557	17 780
30-34	2851	2285	5136	9868	1418	11286	16 422
35-39	3679	2672	6351	9858	1345	11203	17 554
Total	17640	21369	39009	58321	16949	75270	114 279

Abbreviations: Illt. = Illiterate
R & W = Read and write

APPENDIX 7

Breakdown of Male Students by Vocation
at the End of April During Academic Year 1984/1985

Centres for Men

Stage	Nationality	Soldier	Employee	Policeman	Office boy	Public driver	Taxi driver	Messenger	Grocer	Trader	Farmer	Sailor	Carpenter	Mechanic	Mason	Servant	Guardian	Unemployed	Teacher	Other Vocations Worker	Other Vocations Retired	Other Vocations Fireman	TOTAL	GRAND TOTAL
First Inter-mediate	K	113	145	47	5	1	5	11	-	10	-	1	1	3	-	-	37	169	-	18	17	-	583	1645
	NK	662	72	70	8	3	-	5	-	6	1	3	3	7	-	2	14	226	-	16	-	-	1062	1645
Second Inter-mediate	K	119	179	67	1	4	13	10	-	14	3	-	1	2	-	-	21	200	-	17	2	-	653	1543
	NK	512	46	51	5	4	-	7	-	5	-	1	2	2	1	-	3	222	-	29	-	-	890	
Third Inter-mediate	K	139	241	74	1	1	1	13	-	13	-	-	1	1	-	-	7	303	-	21	-	17	833	1535
	NK	377	36	40	3	4	-	3	-	2	2	1	3	3	3	-	7	210	-	8	-	17	702	
Fourth Inter-mediate	K	171	321	91	-	3	4	18	-	25	-	3	-	5	-	-	14	427	-	16	-	-	1098	2086
	NK	539	61	79	3	3	-	5	2	1	-	-	2	4	3	-	8	263	-	15	-	-	988	
Average	K	524	886	279	7	9	23	52	-	62	3	4	3	11	-	-	79	1099	-	72	19	17	3167	6809
Total	NK	2050	219	240	19	14	-	20	2	14	3	5	10	16	7	2	32	921	-	68	-	-	3642	

APPENDIX 8

Breakdown of Female Students by Vocation
at the End of April During Academic Year 1984/1985

Centres for Women

Stage	Kuwaiti	Non-Kuwaiti	Iraqi	Jordanian	Saudi	Egyptian	Syrian	Lebanese	South Yemeni	Somali	North Yemeni	Palestinian	Bahraini	Omani	Qatari	Sudanese	Emirates	Irani	Other Nationalities	Total Non-Kuwaities	GRAND TOTAL
Literacy stage	2035	1322	68	37	134	70	20	2	11	9	7	-	-	1	-	3	-	17	14	1715	3750
Intermediate stage	3444	747	114	61	73	50	15	5	4	3	3	2	4	-	1	1	1	16	18	1118	3562
Secondary stage	2173	221	125	207	47	33	31	24	6	4	5	12	5	5	4	1	2	11	2	735	2908
Total	6652	2290	307	305	253	143	66	31	21	16	15	14	9	6	5	5	3	44	34	3568	10220

Percentage of Female Kuwaities = 65%

APPENDIX 9

Information Map for the Literacy Campaign
During the 1984/1985 Academic Year

General objectives

- Continue information dissemination on the importance of literacy by linking it to development subjects for the individual
and addressing his sense of religion, family and community,
as well as the possibility of improving his functional performance, productivity and the reinforcement of progress.

- Publish the results of the efforts undertaken by state, regional and international organizations in the field of literacy education as well as their impact on improving the cultural, social, health and economic standard.

- Promote the concept of good citizenship in all its dimensions
among individuals, associations and communities in mobilizing
all possible efforts in programmes for cultural awareness,
literacy and adult education.

- Bring to light the problems that may hinder the literacy campaign and make efforts to resolve them in order to encourage
those abstaining from educational programmes, especially
women, to enrol in a literacy centre.

- Point out the achievements of the campaign and the possibilities and incentives offered for literacy and adult education.
Focus on male and female students who have succeeded in the
literacy classes and on the prize-giving day to attract and
encourage enrolment in the centres with an aim to eventually
totally eradicating illiteracy.

APPENDIX 9 (Cont.)

Statistics Based on the Census of the Number of Kuwaiti
Illiterates 15-Years-Old and Above

Years of the general count	Sex	Kuwaities 15-years-old and above	Illiterates 15-years-old and above	%
1957	males	32 581	28 598	87.7
	females	30 167	27 292	90.4
	total	62 748	55 890	89.0
1965	males	56 977	43 535	76.4
	females	59 832	47 325	79.0
	total	116 809	90 860	77.7
1970	males	87 142	57 153	65.5
	females	86 191	70 848	82.1
	total	173 333	128 001	73.8
1975	males	118 529	65 348	55.1
	females	120 117	87 961	73.2
	total	238 646	153 309	64.2
1980	males	140 014	59 187	42.2
	females	147 311	93 389	63.3
	total	287 325	152 576	53.1
1985	males			
	females			
	total			
1990	males			
	females			
	total			

APPENDIX 10

Enactment of Law No. 4 of 1981 Concerning Literacy

- In view of the Emirate decree issued on Ramadan 4, 1936 A.H./ August 29, 1976 to revise the constitution

- In view of the Emirate decree issued on Shawal 14, 1400 A.H./ August 24, 1980

- In view of Law No. 15 of 1979 for civil services

- In view of Law No. 38 of 1964 concerning work in private secotrs, which was revised by Law no. 4 of 1968

- In view of Law No. 11 of 1965 concerning compulsory education

- In view of the proposal made by the Minister of Education

- Following the cabinet's authorization

The following law has been issued:

Article 1

Literacy is a national obligation with the aim of providing education to every member of the society which will help him face life's requirements and will raise the cultural and social level of both the individual and the society.

Article 2

The illiterate is defined as one whose educational level does not meet the standards set by the Minister of Education. The Minister issued the decrees concerning the rules and procedures of the educational level of those who read and write without having obtained a literacy certiticate.

Article 3

Literacy instruction is compulsory for the following:

a) Illiterate Kuwaiti males above the compulsory school age of fourteen years and below forty years old.

APPENDIX 10 (Cont.)

b) Illiterate Kuwaiti females who work in the government sectors and are not yet thirty-five years old. Those who do not fall within the above-mentioned group may voluntarily join the literacy courses. The obligation for literacy education is defined by a Ministerial decree and is gradually diffused in stages according to the groups.

Article 4

The Committee for Literacy Education, headed by the Minister of Education and other members, was formed in order to draw up the general outlines of the literacy policy as well as ratify the work plan which is required in implementing this law. A decree proposed by the Minister is issued for the formation, functions and working methods of this committee.

Article 5

Every ministry, organization, public establishment and private enterprise is committed to implementing the approved working plan for literacy education.

Article 6

The Ministry of Education is responsible for the implementation of the general literacy education policy.

Article 7

The Ministry of Education provides the necessary classes as well as opening classes on the working site for students, pro- vided the owner of the enterprise allows it and the number of students is not less than twenty-five. The Ministry judges that such classes are necessary.

Article 8

Employers are engaged in encouraging workers who fall under the legal obligation for literacy by providing them with literacy classes and giving priority to learning if this should coincide with official work hours.

APPENDIX 10 (Cont.)

Article 9

Literacy education in the centres is offered free of charge, as well as the books, material and educational equipment during the whole literacy course.

Article 10

Every illiterate in the position of literacy obligation must immediately register his or her name in the literacy centre nearest to home or work. The registration must be made within the sixty days following the decree indicated in Article 3, or right after the compulsory rules apply to the illiterate. Students must attend the whole course regularly and sit for all the tests, at the place and time defined by the Ministry of Education. Employers must also submit a list of names of all the personnel working for them during the defined period of sixty days.

Article 11

The Ministry of Education, with the assistance of government sectors, has decided to list all the illiterates falling within the literacy obligation, and register them according to the list as per Article 10 without imposing on them the rules in Article 18.

Article 12

The sick and the handicapped are exempt from this law until the reason for exemption no longer exists. The Minister of Education in agreement with the Minister of Health issued a decree defining the illnesses and handicaps allowed under the exemption.

The obligation for literacy may be postponed for certain persons provided the Minister has authorized the postponement by decree.

Article 13

The Minister of Education sets the tests for learners and the literacy syllabus: a ministerial decree is issued to define the methods of undertaking these tests and the timetable.

APPENDIX 10 (Cont.)

Article 14

Each learner having passed the final literacy test is granted a literacy certificate accredited by the Ministry of Education.

Article 15

The outstanding learners in the literacy classes are granted incentive awards according to the regulations drawn by the Literacy Committee, which may propose the incentives for those who obtained the Literacy Certificate.

Article 16

It is prohibited to employ any illiterate Kuwaiti once this law has gone into effect. Those falling under the law may not be employed in government, organizations or public establishments unless they are registered in a literacy centre. The Council for Civil Services is authorized to exempt from the law those with special circumstances who need to be employed.

Article 17

An illiterate employee may not receive a promotion without holding a literacy certificate as stipulated in Article 14 of this law. When receiving this certificate the promotion is automatically granted as of the date the promotion was offered.

Article 18

Apart from Article 17 of this law, illiterates who have not registered by the deadline will pay a fine of not more than one hundred dinars unless they had a good excuse for not register-ing on time.

Article 19

A student who exceeds a 25% absenteeism rate during the aca-demic year of the literacy classes is fined fifty dinars unless he has a plausible excuse for not attending regularly. The excuses accepted for inattendance are decreed by the Minister.

APPENDIX 10 (Cont.)

Article 20

Enterprise owners who have violated the regulations of Articles 8 and 10 (second part) and Article 17 of this law are penalized with a fine of not more than one hundred dinars which is paid according to the number of workers who fall under obligation of literacy. This fine is doubled if the violation is repeated.

Article 21

The employees appointed by the Ministry for the supervision of the implementation of the law have the right to enter any non-residential building in which they are entitled to check registration books and ledgers to find out cases of violation. They also write an official report concerning any violation and can be assisted by the police in their duty.

Article 22

The Minister of Education issues the necessary decrees for the implementation of the law.

Article 23

With the beginning of the academic year 1981/82 every concerned Minister is to implement the law and abide by it. This is also to be published in the official newspaper.

Gaber Al Ahmed
Emir of Kuwait

Prime Minister: Saad Al Abd Allah Al Sabah

Minister of Education: Gassem Khaled Al Dawed Al Marzouk

Issued at the Seif Palace on January 11, 1981.

REFERENCES

(English translation of the Arabic documents referred to in this study)

1) *General Education Objectives of Kuwait*, March 1976

2) Op. cit. (1)

3) *Statistics and evaluations of the Ministry of Planning, 1984-1985*

4) Op. cit. (3)

5) Op. cit. (3)

6) *Statistics of the Ministry of Education, 1984-1985*

7) Op. cit. (3)

8) *The Education Guidebook of Kuwait*. Planning and Follow-up Department, May 1985

9) *Efforts of Kuwait*. Administration for Adult Education of the Ministry of Education, 1983

10) *A pamphlet on the efforts of Kuwait for literacy and adult education*. The first pamphlet - Permanent Committee for Literacy Education, 1981

11) Op. cit. (10) pp. 30-32

12) *Pamphlet on extracts of the literacy Law No. 4 of 1981 - Second Pamphlet* - the Permanent Information Committee for Literacy, pp. 17 and 51

13) *Efforts of Kuwait in literacy and adult education -* Information Committee, 1985, p. 27

210

REFERENCES (cont.)

14) *Monthly statistics issued for literacy and adult education* - November 1984 - April 1985

15) *Statistical tables of the examination.* Department of the Administration for Adult Education - First term, 1984-1985

16) *Glimpses of the second law for literacy* (a pamphlet), Permanent Committee for Information, 1984, pp. 17-18

17) *Pamphlet on the efforts of Kuwait in literacy and adult education,* Information Committee, 1985. pp. 15-17

18) *Statistics issued by the centres and students concerning the administration of adult education,* 1968

19) *Education guidebook of Kuwait* - Ministry of Education, Planning Department, 1985, p. 26

20) *Arithmetic book - first form literacy stage* - Ministry of Education, 1981- 1982

21) *Arithmetic book - second form literacy stage* - Ministry of Education, 1975-1976

22) *Pamphlet on the nineteenth international day for literacy-* Administration of Adult Education - Kuwait, 1984

23) *Decree number wt/sh 1/7/18047 of 1981 concerning the reorganization of the Administration for Literacy and Adult Education*